BLUEPRINTS FOR BETTER READING

Florence Damon Cleary

Department of School Library Education
Wayne State University, Detroit, Michigan

New York

THE H. W. WILSON COMPANY

1957

BLUEPRINTS
FOR
BETTER
READING

School Programs for Promoting
Skill and Interest in Reading

To

*the hundreds of men and women who have been in
my college classes—a captive audience but a
rewarding one*

PREFACE

No magic formula or design for reading is presented in this book. The author has tried only to identify some of the problems and suggest a variety of plans and procedures that may serve as general guides to members of school staffs who are attempting to help our youth develop skill and interest in reading.

The illustrations, anecdotes, and evaluation materials used by the author were drawn from a number of sources: from her many years of experience as the librarian of a large urban school; from the interview materials, school-staff interaction records, and test data of the Detroit Citizenship Education Study obtained during the five-year period that the author worked with the participating schools as a staff coordinator; and from college classes and curriculum workshops in which she has participated with teachers and librarians as they have defined goals, formulated hypotheses, and tested them in classrooms and school libraries.

This explanation is not offered to defend the point of view expressed in the book, but to indicate that the assumptions and recommendations did not originate full blown from armchair speculation. They evolved from what William James called "knowledge of acquaintance."

The book is designed for two groups of readers. First, for those preparing themselves to teach children, whether in classrooms or libraries, this book offers suggestions that may help them acquire skill in the selection and evaluation of books and other instructional materials; develop understanding of the ways books and reading can become instruments for teaching attitudes and values as well as sources of pleasure and fulfillment; gain insight into the kind of reading guidance that encourages children and youth to develop the spirit of inquiry and the habit of fact finding; and, finally, achieve facility in teaching the skills for finding, organizing, and utilizing information. The book may therefore serve as a supplementary text for library science classes, education classes and curriculum workshops devoted to the study of communication skills, curriculum materials, and the guidance of reading. For this reason Problems for Study and Discussion are included at the end of each chapter.

The book is also designed as a procedural manual and as an "idea book" for practicing teachers, librarians, and administrators. It describes the factors that influence the reading of boys and girls; lists criteria for the evaluation and selection of reading and learning materials in a school and the aids and tools for their selection; indicates the kinds of organization and schedules essential in promoting effective reading guidance programs and the skills required by teachers and librarians in providing effective learning experiences for boys and girls through the medium of books; and lastly offers recommendations and proposals for teaching the learning skills, skills that help promote lasting habits of reading and reflection.

To many people the writer owes debts difficult to assess or acknowledge: the students in library science classes and curriculum workshops at Wayne State University, Detroit, Michigan, and at the State University Teachers College, Geneseo, New York; the donor and the trustees of the Detroit Citizenship Study who made possible the development and collection of much of the data cited in the book. To a number of her colleagues the author expresses special appreciation for their abiding interest and help: Arnold R. Meier, Department of Instructional Research, Detroit Public Schools; Elaine Forsythe Cook, sociologist and author; Alice Damon Rider, Director of the Department of Library Education, State University Teachers College, Geneseo, New York; Thelma E. Hurd, Head of the Language Department, Durfee Junior High School, Detroit, Michigan; and Lois T. Place, Director of School Libraries, Detroit Public Schools. And, finally, a word of thanks to the children with whom the writer has lived at home and in school. From them she has learned how much knowledge, understanding, and delight books provide the individual who has really learned how to read.

FLORENCE DAMON CLEARY

February 1957

CONTENTS

Part II

Programs in Reading Guidance

PART I

FOUNDATIONS OF READING GUIDANCE

Keepers of books, keepers also of the records of the human spirit—the records of men's watch upon the world and on themselves. In such a time as ours, when wars are made against the spirit and its works, the keeping of these records is itself a kind of warfare.

—Archibald MacLeish

CHAPTER 1

ABOUT READERS AND READING:
A POINT OF VIEW

*The mere fact that a person holds a book in his hands . . .
and turns its pages means little or nothing. . . . Such thoughtless
surrender may be agreeable. It may pass the time. . . But
certainly it does not stoke the mind since it leaves the mind
untouched.*

— JOHN MASON BROWN

Considerable discussion of the *'tis, 'tisn't* variety is presently
taking place about the reading of today's youth. Lay people,
parents, and teachers alike are concerned because Johnny can't
read. Librarians are perplexed because Johnny doesn't read.
Research findings and statistics appear to yield contradictory
evidence about reading interests and abilities. Generalizations
are tossed around in a fairly haphazard fashion about the extent
of reading retardation and the reasons for it.

Seldom have professional educators been more defensive or
critics of the schools more vociferous in their assessment of modern methods of teaching. A number of critics oversimplify the
problem to the point of absurdity with such suggestions as, "Teach
the child what each letter stands for and he can read." And a
few professional educators retire to a never-never land of wishful
thinking with the statement that a child reading is a child thinking thoughts.

Such debate demonstrates the importance of books and reading in today's world, but produces few answers to the classroom
teachers and librarians who daily are confronted with the task
of helping boys and girls acquire skill and abiding interest in
reading. How does the individual gain real facility in reading?
What learnings should be provided? What skills acquired? Can
one assume that a child who correctly pronounces all the words

or the child who reads a book a day is inevitably a skillful reader
or even a thoughtful one? Consider these incidents:

The seventh-grade pupils of a school located in an underprivileged
area of a large city were at work on a unit titled Home and Family Living.
A group of girls were designing furniture that could be built at little cost
and were furnishing a model home. Twelve-year-old Sara, one of the
group members, brought the teacher a small cardboard bed that she had
constructed.

"And look, Miss Johnson," she said, "I went to the library yesterday
and got a report on it!"

She held out her paper and Miss Johnson glanced at the title, *Bed*.
She read the first line: *A bed is a layer of stratified rock*. Copied word
for word from an encyclopedia was a concise explanation of the geological
term, *bed*.

Sara had sought and obtained information. She could have
pronounced a majority of the words in the report. The step of
interpretation, the *what do the words mean to me* step, she had
not taken. Neither had she become involved in the process of
relating the ideas presented in the report with the object that she
held in her hand. She had gathered information but had not acquired knowledge. Along with innumerable other children
in this country, Sara lacks skill in reading.

But even more prevalent are the Susies who can't read although they rate high on tests of reading aptitude. The librarian
of the junior high school in an upper-middle class community
was puzzled when she observed Susie, an attractive eighth-grade
girl, pausing to place a mark on the bottom of a page midway
through the book before she returned it to the library circulation
desk. Susie was quick to explain:

"Miss Abbey, we're having a contest in our room to see who will read
the most books this semester. I'm a fast reader so I've already read fifty,
but I never remember what I read. I often get a book half read through
before realizing that I've already read it. Now I put a tiny check on the
bottom of page seventy-eight. When I'm choosing books in the library, all
I have to do to find out if I have read the book is to look on that page."

A classroom teacher had provided a competitive situation in
which little value was placed upon quality, high value on quantity, and the resultant reading activity might be described as in
one eye and out the other. To assume that Susie will become a
skillful reader because she reads a great deal is not in keeping

with research findings that indicate that in the development of skill the individual may become habituated to poor procedures as well as good ones—that practice does not always make perfect.

These incidents bring into sharp focus the problems confronting teachers and librarians as they plan reading programs. On the assumption that reading can be an instrument for lifelong learning, for personal satisfaction and fulfillment, school staffs expend a tremendous amount of energy on reading guidance. Books and other curriculum materials are made available in school and classroom libraries. School administrators organize developmental reading programs and encourage all their teachers to become reading teachers. Reading lists are developed. Readings are assigned. Young people do reference work in the library and give reports in classes. Special classes are maintained for retarded readers. Librarians teach the use of books and libraries. Voluntary reading is encouraged and rewarded.

The results of these efforts are often disquieting. While it is true that many pupils acquire high interest and efficiency in reading, far too many young people who make up typical school populations become increasingly uninterested and hostile as, grade by grade, they are forced to pursue more and more unintelligible materials. This generalization appears to be well bolstered by research.

In a survey of the reading interests of over 5,000 children in the midwest Witty found that 95 per cent of the pupils in grades one through five reported liking to read. A marked decline began in the sixth grade where 81 per cent gave an affirmative reaction, a decline that continued in the upper grades.[1]

In a study of leisure reading interests Sheldon and Cutts found that "almost half of the above average and the superior readers have reading as an out of school interest or hobby, . . . about one fourth of the average and only one tenth of the below-average readers seem to be interested in reading at home."[2]

[1] Paul A. Witty and David Kopel, "Studies of the Activities and Preferences of School Children," *Educational Administration and Supervision*, XXIV (September 1938), 434.

[2] William D. Sheldon and Warren C. Cutts, "Relation of Parents, Home and Certain Developmental Characteristics to Children's Reading Ability," *Elementary School Journal*, LIII (May 1953), 517-21.

From the findings of other surveys, it appears that from 15 to 20 per cent of high school pupils are seriously retarded in reading ability,[3] and that 13.5 per cent of adults over twenty-five years of age are functionally illiterate since their reading ability is below fourth-grade level.[4] Norvell concluded from his study of the reading interests of high school youth in the state of New York that over half the selections read by them in literature classes ranked low in interest.[5]

While it is true that surveys of adult reading habits give contradictory reactions regarding the amount and quality of the reading done by the average American, a number of carefully documented studies provide evidence to show that nearly two thirds of the adult population may be considered non-readers of books; that 75 per cent of the books published are read by 5 per cent of the people; that public library card holders comprise only 25 per cent of the adult population and only 10 per cent use the library as often as once a month; that pulp magazines and news-papers are the major sources of reading material;[6] and that the general effect of the reading done by many adults is aptly described by Edgar Dale when he states that while reading, like television, may help to mature people, it may also arrest them at an infantile level of development.[7]

Taking into account the vast outpouring of printed informa-tion, and the need for people to understand and to share meanings with others, it seems fair to assume that teachers and librarians everywhere must conclude: However well we have done in the past, we can do better. We need to provide more effective, re-warding reading experiences for children and youth.

[3] Paul A. Witty and David Kopel, *Reading and the Educative Process* (Boston Ginn & Company, 1939), p. 11-12.

[4] David H. Russell, *Children Learn to Read* (Boston: Ginn & Co., 1949), p. 5.

[5] George Norvell, *The Reading Interests of Young People* (Boston: D. C. Heath & Co., 1950), p. 84.

[6] Lester Asheim, "What Do Adults Read?" *Adult Reading*, edited by Nelson B. Henry. The Fifty-fifth Yearbook of the National Society for the Study of Education, Part 2 (Chicago: University of Chicago Press, 1954), pp. 5-27.

[7] Edgar Dale, "The Challenge of Audio-Visual Media," in *Challenges to Librarian-ship*, ed. by Louis Shores. (Tallahassee: Florida State University, 1953), p. 104.

BASIC ASSUMPTIONS

During the past few years the following significant concepts have become increasingly clear. They suggest a philosophical base which school staffs might use to evaluate present reading programs and to plan for improvement.

1. Reading can be a potent factor in the development of the knowledge, understandings, appreciations, values, and beliefs required by the individual in dealing with his own problems and in relating himself effectively with others. Reading, however, is a complicated skill, and the degree to which a high potential is attained by pupils depends on the teacher's understanding of the specific values in books; on his understanding of the motivations, drives, and interests of his pupils; and on his skill in encouraging young people to read and to generalize from their reading, to relate and apply the values in many situations and associations.

2. There should be no assumption that boys and girls in the middle and upper grades have learned to read and hence have no further need for reading guidance in the content subjects. Reading the words is a basic skill, but discovering what the words mean, relating ideas, utilizing and applying the knowledge gained *is* skill in reading. Moreover, there are a number of intermediate skills such as skimming, outlining, note-taking, reporting, that are essential in the gathering and utilization of knowledge. These are not acquired by chance. They must be taught.

3. The idea that the child will learn to read by reading and that he will develop interest in books if they are made accessible to him is no longer acceptable. School administrators, librarians, and teachers must continue their efforts to provide reading materials that meet the needs and interests of their pupils. Exposure to books and other nondirective reading guidance techniques are sufficient motivations for numbers of children. For still larger numbers, reading periods in the classroom or library, when little

guidance is given, produce neither interest nor skill. Librarians and teachers must provide real learning situations, taking into account such viewpoints about learning as readiness, relatedness, and usefulness of learning experiences.

4. Skill and interest must be considered interdependent factors in the development of reading tastes and habits. The skillful reader tends to develop and maintain high interest in reading. In turn, high interest motivates the development of greater skill. In planning reading programs teachers and librarians tend to consider these two factors as mutually exclusive. They make a sharp distinction between free, voluntary, or recreational reading, and required or reference reading. The attendant result of compartmentalizing reading, of labeling and categorizing reading activities is that pupils sometimes gain the impression that free or recreational reading is interesting, while reading for information is dull and difficult.

5. Reading does not at present stand in danger of becoming obsolete although people increasingly are entertained and informed by such mass media of communication as television, radio, movies, the newsreels, tabloids, comics, and pictorial magazines. These media may be competitive users of time but they cannot provide in the way that books do the complete record of man's best thinking or the story of his cultural heritage. Moreover, the symbols on the pages of a book are not fleeting and evanescent. The reader may proceed at his own rate, may pause to reflect, to question, to clarify his thinking, to weigh his own values, to agree or disagree. Thus for the skillful reader, books can be a charging of mind and spirit, a pleasure that needs no defense or explanation.

Events of the past several years lend urgency to the task of improving our skills in communicating and participating with others in all of life's complex associations. During the past few years hundreds of studies and projects have been initiated to find better ways of teaching the youth of America how to acquire these understandings and skills. Many of these are taking place in classrooms or in individual schools, others in school systems and school communities. Some involve attempts to improve citizenship, human relations, and mental health; others in finding out how children grow and learn. Hundreds have been devoted, primarily, to a study of communication skills.

In a considerable number of these undertakings participating school staffs have become involved in evaluating the materials of instruction and in seeking ways to improve their reading guidance programs. They have developed specific criteria for the selection and use of books and learning materials, criteria that emphasize the developmental values in books and that take into account the culture patterns and the abilities and needs of particular pupils. They have deliberately used books, fiction and non-fiction, to teach an understanding of the democratic values and skill in human relationships. They have encouraged children to read books related to their problems and concerns, to generalize from their reading, and to test their findings in actual every-day situations. They have sought to develop the spirit of inquiry and the habit of fact finding and have taught the skills required for finding and using information in the solving of problems. They have never deviated from the idea that children should read for enjoyment, yet they have come to see that possibly this should be a by-product rather than a major objective of the reading program.

These approaches are not new or extraordinary. Their uniqueness lies in the way that librarians and teachers have formulated specific objectives, have planned reading guidance programs consistent with those objectives and evaluated results. To tell the story of their experiences is the major purpose of this book.

Part I tells of the understandings and skills required of the person who selects the materials and guides the reading of youth. It describes the school organization and procedures that facilitate effective guidance programs.

Part II explores and describes a variety of approaches to reading guidance: the programs that place emphasis on the tasks and concerns of children; the teaching procedures for helping them to read critically; and the organized assistance provided by skillful teachers and librarians that boys and girls may learn to love to read because they have really learned how.

PROBLEMS FOR DISCUSSION AND STUDY

1. As you read this book you will observe that the writer believes in the idea that reading activities should never be considered as busy work or as a kind of time filler or time killer. The child learns something from every experience he has under the guidance of the school and, if he learns to dislike reading, it may be assumed that experiences provided have not met his needs and purposes. The five assumptions given in the previous chapter are based on this point of view. If you do not agree with them, try to formulate a number of other assumptions on which you would prefer to build a reading program.

2. Discuss and explore the status of reading in the United States, using such sources as *Library Literature, Education Index,* and *Readers' Guide to Periodical Literature* to locate reports of recent studies and surveys.

3. If you are currently employed in a school either as a teacher or librarian, outline in some detail your school's reading program. How would you evaluate its effectiveness?

4. Whether you are a teacher or librarian, you will read this book because you are looking for ways to improve your teaching of children. It is hoped, however, that you will read critically, agreeing or disagreeing with expressed points of view—using as criteria your own purposes, saying to yourself, What learnings do I want for my pupils? What learnings are they acquiring as a result of the reading experiences they are having in the school? Are there suggestions made in this book that I can try out and evaluate?

OTHER SUGGESTED READINGS

Berelson, Bernard. *The Library's Public.* New York: Columbia University Press, 1949.

Center, Stella S. *The Art of Book Reading.* New York: Charles Scribner's Sons, 1953.

Gray, William S. *Reading in an Age of Mass Communication; Report of the Committee on Reading of the National Council of Teachers of English.* New York: Appleton-Century-Crofts, 1949.

Gray, William S. "Summary of Reading Investigations, July 1, 1953— June 30, 1954." *Journal of Educational Research,* XLVIII (February 1955), 401-442.

Gray, William S. "Summary of Reading Investigations, July 1, 1954— June 30, 1955." *Journal of Educational Research,* XLIX (February 1956), 401-436.

Hazard, Paul. *Books, Children and Men.* Boston: Horn Book Inc., 1947.

Johnson, Elmer D. *Communication.* New Brunswick, N.J.: Scarecrow Press, 1955.

Link, H. C. and Hopf, H. A. *People and Books: A Study of Reading and Book Buying Habits.* New York: Book Industry Committee, Book Manufacturers' Institute, 1946.

Marshall, John D. and others, comps. *Books, Libraries, Librarians.* Hamden, Conn.: Shoe String Press, 1955.

National Society for the Study of Education. *Adult Reading.* Fifty-fifth Yearbook, Part 2. Chicago: University of Chicago Press, 1956.

National Society for the Study of Education. *Mass Media and Education.* Fifty-third Yearbook, Part 2. Chicago: University of Chicago Press, 1954.

Schramm, Wilbur, ed. *Communications in Modern Society.* Urbana: University of Illinois Press, 1948.

Shores, Louis, ed. *Challenges to Librarianship.* Tallahassee: Florida State University, 1953.

Stefferud, Alfred, ed. *The Wonderful World of Books.* New York: Houghton Mifflin Co., 1952.

Traxler, A. E. and Townsend, Agatha. *Eight More Years of Research in Reading.* New York: Educational Records Bureau, 1955.

Witty, Paul A. *Reading and Modern Education.* Boston: D. C. Heath & Co., 1949.

CHAPTER 2

UNDERSTANDING CHILDREN AND
THE FACTORS THAT INFLUENCE
THEIR READING

*He who helps a child helps humanity with a distinctness, with
an immediateness, which no other help given to human creatures
in any other stage of their human life can possibly give again.*
— PHILLIPS BROOKS

*You cannot stare over an adult high fence—not even a white-
washed, nine foot, Mark Twain fence—and get back into the
essence of childhood.*
— MEINDERT DE JONG

Miss Smith's kindergarten pupils were making their first
visit to the school library. Arranged on the library tables, open
and inviting, were numbers of books. *Cock-a-Doodle-Doo,*[1] *Flip
and the Cows,*[2] *The Little Wild Horse,*[3] *Farm Stories,*[4] *The Wonderful Feast,*[5] and several others gay with pictures of tractors,
cowbarns, and farmers at work. The children seated themselves
on the floor in a semicircle around the librarian and listened with
breathless attention to the adventures of *The Little Old Truck,*[6]
crowding closer to look at the pictures.

Hardly had the librarian read the last sentence before the
five-year-olds were all talking at once about the pick-up trucks

[1] Berta (Hoerner) Hader and Elmer Hader, *Cock-a-Doodle-Doo;* the story of a
little red rooster (New York: Macmillan Co., 1939).

[2] Wesley Dennis, *Flip and the Cows;* the story and pictures by Wesley Dennis
(New York: Viking Press, 1942).

[3] Hetty Burlingame Beatty, *The Little Wild Horse* (Boston: Houghton Mifflin
Co., 1949).

[4] Kathryn Jackson, *Farm Stories* by K. and B. Jackson, with pictures by Gustaf
Tenggren (New York: Simon & Schuster, 1946).

[5] Esphyr Slobodkina, *The Wonderful Feast* (New York: Lothrop, Lee & Shepard
Co., 1955).

[6] Jay Hyde Barnum, *The Little Old Truck;* story and pictures by Jay Hyde
Barnum (New York: William Morrow & Co., 1953).

they had at home, for these children lived on farms in upstate New York. They had traveled long distances by bus to the new central school and the first days had been strange and a little frightening. In the story they found familiar surroundings and incidents and, as they related their own experiences, cheerfulness pervaded the school library. Feelings of anxiety and strangeness disappeared as books opened doors into a familiar and exciting world.

The librarian would not in all likelihood continue to read farm stories to these small boys and girls. Soon they would meet *The Chinese Children Next Door*,[7] and *The Biggest Bear*.[8] But for their first library hour the librarian had started where the children were. She was aware that children do not come to school or to their early reading experiences empty-handed. They bring with them their families and communities, their concerns and interests, their aptitudes, values, and motivations.

All these factors she had taken into account as she chose the books and planned the learning experience. To the average observer, the "library hour" looked effortless and casual. The librarian was enjoying books with children. In reality she was providing a meaningful and effective learning situation for a unique group of children. Would she have used farm books had she not known the interests and needs of her pupils? Probably not.

The illustration pin-points a problem. Do successful school librarians and teachers know more about their pupils than unsuccessful ones? Does such information tend to make them more sympathetic, more objective in their approaches to children? Are teachers more skillful in devising useful and meaningful learning procedures, more skillful in selecting books and other learning materials if they have background information about each child? Will such efforts take too much time and energy in proportion to the inherent values? For without a doubt the task confronting

[7] Pearl Buck, *The Chinese Children Next Door*, drawings by William Arthur Smith (New York: John Day Co., 1942).

[8] Lynd Kendall Ward, *The Biggest Bear* (Boston: Houghton Mifflin & Co., 1952).

a school staff in knowing and understanding their pupils is time-consuming and the values to be achieved should be carefully assessed.

Some teachers and librarians maintain they want no background knowledge about their pupils since such information makes it difficult for them "to consider children innocent till they prove themselves guilty." In their judgment the adults who know their subject fields and use skillful classroom procedures have little trouble in teaching children. Getting to know individuals, they insist, is not essential.

A similar attitude is taken by some authorities in the field of children's literature who assume that all children will enjoy beautiful books if they are exposed to them. Consequently, it is more important for the person giving guidance to know books than children. They deplore the "mechanistic approach" of some teachers to reading guidance where major consideration is given to meeting individual abilities and needs of the pupil.

Librarians in many public libraries who see only the children who come voluntarily to the library tend to take this same position, as do many school librarians who work only with middle-class children. A majority of these pupils appear to have spontaneous interest and love for reading. They present few behavior problems in the library. They enjoy almost any book to which they are exposed. Hence the need to know and to understand the background of these pupils in providing adequate guidance appears less acute, although no less real.

But well over 50 per cent of American youth come from homes of rather limited socio-economic backgrounds. They live in tension areas in large cities where experience tends to make them suspicious and aggressive. The motivations provided by their environment do not encourage reading. It is these children who often greet the "best literature for children" with boredom if not outright cynicism, who reject the book recommendations of teachers, who actively dislike most of the selections pursued in literature classes in the high school.

These young people need more dynamic, useful, and realistic reading experiences in school if they are to become effective readers, and the crucial question confronting school staffs is this: Do teachers who know and understand their pupils and use this information as a basis for planning tend to provide more rewarding relationships and more meaningful and realistic learning in the classroom and library than those who do not?

Reporting his study of teacher-pupil relationships, Robert Bush writes:

> The teachers who know most about their pupils and are aware of and sympathize with their individual needs and interests have effective relationships with a larger number than do teachers whose major concern is subject matter.[9]

Findings from the Detroit Citizenship Study support somewhat similar generalizations. Teachers and librarians who participated in the Study found that as they came to understand the forces that influence growth and learning and motivate behavior, they tended to accept all children perceptively and to be more skillful in establishing deep and rewarding relationships with them. They discovered that as they gained skill in generalizing from the background information about their pupils, they became more effective in planning reading experiences geared to the pupils' needs and abilities.[10]

The available evidence spells out the benefits of knowing one's pupils and understanding the factors that influence their reading, and makes the effort involved in acquiring these understandings appear worth while.

THE FACTORS INFLUENCING THE CHILD'S READING

It can be assumed that the teacher and librarian take the first steps in knowing and understanding their pupils when they collect background information. Yet the task of building cumu-

---

[9] Robert Nelson Bush, *The Teacher-Pupil Relationship* (New York: Prentice-Hall, 1954), p. 180.

[10] Arnold R. Meier and others, *A Curriculum for Citizenship* (Detroit: Wayne University Press, 1952), pp. 291-292.

lative and anecdotal records on each child appears overwhelming for school librarians and special teachers who often have contacts with hundreds of pupils. Short cuts must be found. One effective procedure which will be discussed later in the chapter is the use of questionnaires, checklists, and study forms for gathering information about pupils. Another extremely effective method for gaining insight and understanding is to explore and utilize the research relating to the factors that influence growth and learning, and in turn, the reading of children and youth. In succeeding pages, a number of these findings together with their implications for reading guidance are summarized.

The Impact of the Culture on Learning and Behavior

The social class into which a child is born is a tremendous factor in his personality development since his attitudes and values develop as a result of continued interaction between his inherited potentialities and his environment. Studies reveal marked social class differences in the early training of children which in turn have marked effect on their eating and sleeping habits, their language patterns, their interests, values, motivations, and drives. Allison Davis makes this statement: "We can no longer generalize about the child. We shall have to ask a child in what social class, in what cultural environment." [11]

Findings from research indicate, moreover, that general intelligence tests do not accurately reflect the native capacity, "the mother wit," of the lower class child. Davis maintains that schools which place too much reliance on intelligence quotients tend to provide such meager and poorly motivated learning experiences for these children that society loses the resources of well over half of its people, since over 50 per cent of the children in the public elementary schools come from homes in the lower socioeconomic brackets.

The behavior of these children, which is a perfectly rational response to their home and community life, is often strange and

[11] Allison Davis, *Social Class Influences Upon Learning* (Cambridge: Harvard University Press, 1948), p. 12.

sometimes shocking to the teacher with middle class values and patterns of behavior. The teacher needs, therefore, to understand his own cultural patterns and be sensitive to the cultural patterns of his pupils lest he penalize the child whose home and community background makes the rate of upward mobility slow. This does not mean that the teacher condones poor behavior. He understands it. He must keep the lines of communication open with his pupils. They need his understanding and approval. He needs their confidence.

Very little reading is done in lower class homes. Few books are purchased, few magazines subscribed to. Comics and tabloid newspapers are read, but reading as a leisure activity is not held highly in these homes. The influence of the home on the reading of children is reported in the clinical studies of Sheldon and Carrillo. Evidence collected from parents revealed that such aspects as the following influenced the quality and amount of reading done by youth: the size and social position of the family, the educational level of the parents, and parental interests and hobbies.[12]

The implications of these findings are clearcut. In reading guidance the teacher and librarian need to take careful stock of the culture patterns of their pupils, recognizing that these patterns influence the values, interests, motivations, and behavior of youth. They need to provide books that have meaning and reality for children. They need to develop the close and rewarding relationships that often provide the best motivations that children have for learning, namely, the liking and regard for the teacher. Without real rapport between child and teacher reading guidance will fail, as fail it should.

Conditions for Effective Learning

Findings from studies of the past decade on how children learn provide compelling evidence to teachers and librarians of the need for them to take into strict account such factors and

[12] William D. Sheldon and Lawrence Carrillo, "Relation of Parents, Home and Certain Developmental Characteristics to Children's Reading," *Elementary School Journal*, LII (January 1952), 262-70.

viewpoints about learning as reality, usefulness, interest, and relatedness in planning learning experiences for their pupils. To illustrate: In presenting a new learning to the child the teacher should attempt to identify some kind of problem real to the child so that he will see some use for the learning. The teacher should capitalize on the learner's present interests and potential ones. He should try to relate the new learning to something already known. The child needs to see a clear relationship between his own goals and what he is asked to do in school. The new learning should lead to the achievement of generalizations. At least, the pupil should see some meaning, reality or use for the new learning.

If it can be assumed that one reads to learn and since the purpose of reading guidance is to promote learning, then it follows that the teacher and librarian should take these factors into account in planning the reading experiences they provide for their pupils whether it is an hour in which pupils read for information or one devoted to story telling or reading aloud. The following report of a "story hour" in a school library illustrates what happens when conditions for effective learning are not provided.

The school librarian picked up a book and announced to her fifth-grade class that she would read them a Japanese folk tale titled *The Sun Goddess*. She obviously liked the children who were seated around her in the attractive, well-equipped library. She enjoyed the story. She read it well. About half the class listened with steadfast attention.

The others were not so involved. Some were staring vacantly out the wide library windows. Several boys, from their whispered conversation, appeared to be sharing some information on rocket ships. Two or three pupils were poking nearby classmates while keeping an eye on the librarian to ascertain how much excess activity was advisable. One boy looked over the shoulder of another at a comic book strategically placed in an open notebook. A few looked bored, but resigned. They were passive listeners.

The librarian timed the story carefully with frequent glances at the clock. She read the final sentence as the bell rang announcing the end of the period. As she closed the book, she said, "Did you like the story?" No answer was required, for the boys and girls were passing in fairly orderly fashion out the library door on their way to the next class.

The librarian sincerely wished her pupils to love books. Systematic in her attempts to introduce books and determined not to spoil books for them by too much interpretation and discussion, she had in her presentation violated practically all the well established viewpoints about how children learn. She had provided no incentive for listening, explained no new concepts or ideas in the story. On a table in the library stood a Japanese pottery vase bearing the motif of the chained sun goddess, but she had not commented on it. Neither had she provided a time schedule that made discussion or generalizations possible. She believed that listening to stories was one of the best ways to encourage children to love books, so she read the story. The result was little learning and less enjoyment for well over half of the class.

A child will not enjoy reading when he brings little experience to it, when he sees no purpose for reading; no reality in the content, when he has little opportunity to talk about it. Unless teachers and librarians plan reading experiences that are, first of all, effective learning situations, the child will probably not learn to like to read, though easily accessible to him are books that are the heritage of childhood. In a school where this is happening to large numbers of children, the resulting condition is a lack of interest in reading—a "who cares," "what's the use" atmosphere which does not make for the development of wholesome attitudes towards reading or learning.

The Influence of Growth Patterns

Extensive research has been carried on in the past two decades in an attempt to learn how the individual grows and develops. Findings from studies made at the Iowa Welfare Research Station; the Child Development Institute of Teachers College, Columbia; the Yale Studies; the Harvard Growth Studies, and others, provide conclusive evidence that growth is a matter of individual unfolding. Hence children may have quite different patterns of growth and development. In other words, each individual grows from where he is and not from some predetermined starting point held in common with others. On the basis of this evidence, consideration of individual differences is of crucial importance in all teaching-learning situations.

The research shows, however, that from infancy to adulthood, the child tends to go through a series of sequences in growth. It is possible, therefore, to identify predominant patterns of behavior or typical characteristics of children at certain stages of development. Teachers who are concerned because thirteen- to fifteen-year-old girls giggle, have crushes, are boy-crazy, affect ugly modes of dress, and dislike adult authority are observing completely rational behavior for that age group. It is a stage of development.

Corey and Herrick define the stages of development from infancy through adolescence as developmental tasks that the child needs to accomplish "because of his emerging capacities for action and relationship, because of the demands and expectations of his family and society, and because of the directive power of his own interest, attitudes, values and aspirations." [13]

Havighurst suggests that these developmental tasks arise at or about a certain period of the individual's life and that if they are not achieved, they make the achievement of later tasks difficult and hence block normal maturity. He formulated a rather extensive list of developmental needs and tasks—the need of the little child to win his place in a group, to learn how to give and receive affection, to acquire skill in communication, to find emotional release through sensory experiences; the need of the child in later childhood to deepen and broaden intellectual concepts, to develop further the physical skills, to maintain a role in the peer group; the need of the adolescent to come to terms with his own body, to learn new relationships with his age mates, to develop a scale of values.[14]

Studies in frustration and aggression indicate that when these needs and drives are not met, when over a long period of time children live in an environment where it is impossible for them to work toward the achievement of these tasks, they will have difficulty in making satisfactory adjustment. They may become

[13] Stephen M. Corey and Virgil E. Herrick, "The Developmental Tasks of Children and Young People," in *Youth, Communication and Libraries*, ed. by Frances Henne (Chicago: American Library Association, 1949), p. 3.

[14] Robert J. Havighurst, *Human Development and Education* (New York: Longmans, Green & Co., 1953), p. 1-5.

hostile or openly aggressive or they may withdraw and become unsocial or antisocial.

The implications of these findings are clear. The teacher and the librarian need to foster warm, close relationships with children that provide them with the kind of secure and orderly environment in which the pupil can solve his own problems and work toward the achievement of his developmental tasks.

Since the child tends to identify with book characters, he should be given many experiences with books in which the characters are confronted with developmental tasks similar to his own. Reading programs therefore should be planned with due consideration of how children grow and develop and with painstaking analysis of the developmental values in books.

The Effect of Interest

The role of interest in learning is so decisive that educators are seeking by every means at their command to gain information and insight into children's interests and "what those interests suggest for education." Interest plays a decisive role in the learning and development of the individual, and his talents, abilities, drives, and motivations affect his interests and, in turn, are affected by them. In other words interest motivates learning and learning produces interest. It is a two-way street. Wide variation in interests exists within a group of children and from group to group. Interests change as society changes. Communities breed unique interests. City children, for example, have quite different ones from those in rural communities. Culture patterns, age, sex, and intelligence affect individual interests. The developmental process itself produces changes in interests as the individual matures. In early childhood interests are extensive, evanescent, and shifting. During adolescence individual and sex differences are more marked, and interests become more complex and vigorous; while in adulthood they gradually become more restricted and individualistic.

Considerable data have been collected identifying play preferences, leisure time pursuits, reading and vocational interests and hobbies, and predominant interests at various age levels. The young child's interest in animals and pets, in make believe, in play; the interest of the nine- and ten-year-olds in sports and adventure, mystery, and magic; the young adolescent's interest in people, particularly of his own age group, in vocational choices, and in the opposite sex, are all indicative of the predominant interest patterns of children and youth.

Since interests are crucial factors in learning, how can the schools foster their development? Jersild points out that there is a wide difference between the interests the child acquires and those he might acquire, since what the child likes to do is influenced by what he has had the opportunity to do. He suggests, moreover, that interests are not alone guides or aids to learning, but are forms of experience through which the child discovers his own potentialities. Therefore, teachers must not limit or stereotype his interests by what they think he should be interested in. Instead, the school must deliberately provide the learning of many varied interests so that the child may choose one best suited and most useful to him. This does not mean that there is magic in numbers. The crucial factor relates to the way the individual's interests function and the needs they serve.[15]

The implications of this research for reading guidance are particularly significant since the individual's interests so largely determine what he will read, the amount he reads, and the intensity with which he pursues it. In planning reading activities and in selecting books, teachers and librarians need to take into strict account what is known about predominant interest patterns of children and youth at different age levels as well as the factors that influence those interests since reading interests tend to be but the reflection of general interests.

The librarian who understands, for example, the wide differences in the interests of boys and girls during adolescence will not choose for group reading activities stories of family life, love stories, and girls' stories since adolescent boys reject these stories

[15] Arthur T. Jersild and Ruth J. Tasch, *Children's Interests and What They Suggest for Education* (New York: Bureau of Publications, Teachers College, Columbia University, 1948), pp. 71-87.

completely. Instead he will choose materials that reflect interests common to both adolescent boys and girls, such as sports, science, adventure, and mystery.

Summaries of hundreds of surveys and studies of children's reading interests, the factors that influence reading, their choices in books and magazines are available in current educational literature. Such data are exceedingly helpful, yet they serve only as general guides since reading interests tend to be individualistic and for that reason teachers and librarians need to collect information on their own pupils. Although it is wise to capitalize on the young person's current interests, the teacher and librarian will do well to build bridges from current interests to potential ones. Carried to a logical conclusion this suggests that they put into the child's hands the books he doesn't know he wants as well as those he asks for.

The Influence of Mass Media of Communication

The impact of television, radio, movies, comics, and other mass media of communication on youth is a subject of widespread interest and concern. That they are effective tools of learning, that they affect behavior are widely accepted generalizations. They combine sight and sound to offer action, adventure, excitement, danger, and violence. They place few demands on reading ability. Movies and television, especially, compel attention because in a darkened room that obliterates distractions, the eye is focused on a lighted screen.

Television. What kind of learning experiences are offered the child through these media? On television, unless some kind of selection process is undertaken, the child sees fights and brawls, murders and corpses and smoking guns. He sees, as well, many programs of excellent quality—circuses, puppet shows, animated cartoons, and music. He sees events as they happen. The world is brought to his very door. Studies show that the average twelve- and thirteen-year-old who has a TV set at home spends about thirty hours a week in front of the screen, and the learning he acquires is not easily calculated. Proof of its influence on children's values is the following incident:

A three-year-old girl, with a face like "the littlest angel," her hand holding tightly to her mother's, talked to Santa Claus in the department store's Toyland. "And what do you want Santa to bring you for Christmas?" asked Santa. Kathy was quick to reply: "A two-gun holster like Roy Rogers and a sword so I can chop people."

The possibilities of TV beggar description. For influencing public opinion, for bringing insight and understanding of world events, for clarifying the processes of government, no other medium so effectively combines sight and sound. And the use of educational TV is still in its infancy.

Movies. While it is true that TV has reduced movie attendance, the lines of children in front of movie houses on Saturday and Sunday afternoons are sufficiently long to discredit the idea that movies are no longer popular or influential with children and youth. Although written and produced for adults, movies are still "youth's most popular story book." Reflecting life in exaggerated form as they often do, they are swallowed, the unreal along with the real, by juveniles who do not know the difference. That they often give an erroneous picture of life to youth, that they affect adversely the troubled and delinquent child appear to matter not at all to many parents if one accepts the evidence from the surveys as to the scarcity of parent supervision of the movie attendance of their children.

In contrast, the widespread use of educational movies, films, and filmstrips in school rooms across the country attests to their value as learning aids. They build experiences and promote understandings. They present meanings, heighten reality and may, if used effectively by teachers, change attitudes and values. If "one picture is worth a hundred words," then their influence on the learning of children is incalculable.

Radio. Radio, like other media of communication, suffered with the advent of television, but, like the movies, it is far from obsolete. Recent surveys reveal surprising trends. A large majority of high school youth report listening to radio from two to four hours daily. True, the most popular programs are the disc jockeys, and a high percentage of listening goes on while homework and other activities are being pursued.

Few commercial programs can be called educational. Yet, if radio needs any defense as an effective medium of communication, its supporters can point to the network of radio stations owned and operated by school systems. Day by day programs are wired into the schools where, if properly motivated and used by classroom teachers, they become valid learning experiences for youth.

Comics. Another medium, one which combines visual techniques with print, cannot be ignored in an evaluation of the effect of mass communication media on youth. Over 90 million comic books are entering American homes each month and are being read by an estimated 70 million children of widely differing cultural backgrounds and intelligence quotients. Researchers estimate that 95 per cent of boys, 91 per cent of girls, from 6 to 11, and 87 per cent of boys, 81 per cent of girls, ages 12 to 17 read them regularly.[16]

The popularity of comic books may be described as a social phenomenon. Government and industry use them in personnel training with marked success. Children return home from church carrying Bible story comics instead of the traditional Sunday School lesson leaflets. Comic books are the most popular reading of our armed forces. Their appeal is not difficult to assess. Action starts immediately and proceeds with supersonic speed. The pictures tell the story. Moreover, comic books are easily accessible and cost little.

Until recently most educators have expressed no great anxiety regarding the harmful effects of comic books on the child. While they agree that comics often portray unrealistic adventures and false values, that the art is atrocious and the taste questionable, they have recognized their appeal and have held the belief that, if comics are not prohibited to the average child, he will enjoy them for a time and then proceed to more worth-while reading experi-

[16] Paul A. Witty and R. A. Sizemore, "Reading the Comics, a Summary of Studies and an Evaluation," *Elementary English*, XXXI (December 1954), 501-6.

ences. In fact, a few authorities still hold the position that "good comics" should be encouraged since they furnish a foundation on which an interest in finer literature may be built. Moreover they give the retarded reader material he can enjoy, and the child with serious behavior problems a sense of adventure and release.

More recently, however, the evidence against the comics has been piling up. Numbers of adults whose learning and development have been arrested at immature levels are constant readers of comics, and research is being attempted to discover if there are any cause-and-effect relationships. In his study of comics Fredric Wertham maintains that "the good comics are snowed under by those glorifying violence, crime and sadism." He would ban all comics as he believes the less objectionable ones initiate the child into this type of reading. His findings indicate that the stimulation and seduction of the comics are decisive factors in the maladjustments of large numbers of youth. He paints a disquieting picture of the effects, which he insists go far beyond that imagined by adults.[17]

A good many juvenile court authorities, also, are convinced that a large number of crimes committed by youth appear to be motivated in good measure by horror comics. Although the damaging effects of the comics is cause for concern, banning them by legal procedures is a first step in curtailing freedom of the press, and other means for their control appear the more feasible. The voluntary action of book publishers in signing a code of ethics relating to the sale of comics appears to be a wise approach to the problem.

The Effect of Mass Media on Reading. Influential as are all these media—radio, TV, movies, and comics—in the lives of a young person, do they affect adversely the use he makes of print? Have the amount and quality of his reading changed noticeably and, if so, can these changes be traced to his transcending concentration on other media? Findings from available studies are somewhat contradictory. Yet it is evident that mass media

[17] Fredric Wertham, *The Seduction of the Innocent* (New York: Rinehart & Co., 1953).

influence markedly both the quantity and quality of youth's reading.

During the first six months of TV ownership, families spend a high percentage of their leisure in television viewing. In 1952, Paul Witty surveyed over two thousand elementary children in Evanston, Illinois. Thirty-nine per cent of the respondents reported that their reading had decreased since television and that they preferred television to reading.[18] Other surveys made at that time revealed startling figures of thirty to fifty hours a week spent by children in watching programs. School authorities in several cities reported homework undone and children asleep at their desks at ten in the morning. Surveys revealed heavy losses in the numbers of children's books circulated by both school and public libraries.

More recently it has appeared that the viewing time of children is greatly reduced and that they are returning more and more to reading and other leisure interests. In fact, television may actually promote reading. The tremendous upsurge of interest in science books, fiction and non-fiction, is traceable to interest stimulated by TV programs, and many school and public librarians report a tremendous increase in requests for books and other printed materials about subjects presented on TV programs.

To a lesser degree the movies also appear to stimulate an interest in reading. Libraries report heavy circulation of books made into movies. Currently adults as well as children are requesting Verne's *Twenty Thousand Leagues Under the Sea* and the stories of Hans Christian Andersen.

What are the implications for reading guidance in what has been learned about the effects of mass media of communication? A number of observations are suggested:

> These media greatly enlarge the child's world as they provide knowledge and information and open doors to new interests. The broader the child's experiential background— the more he brings to his reading—the greater will his interest in reading tend to be.

[18] Paul A. Witty, "Comparative Studies of Interest in T. V.," *Educational Administration and Supervision*, XL (October 1954), 321-25.

Since these media affect the child's interests and since his reading interests are but reflections of his general interests, skillful teachers and librarians will exploit to the full all communication media. This means that they need to have real familiarity with all these media and use them as bona fide learning experiences in the school room.

Possibly the most damaging effect of these media is their stifling of creative and imaginative pursuits. Children tend to become watchers rather than investigators and initiators, a situation that may well cause concern to parents and educators. The field of imaginative literature may be an antidote.

Assuming that no other medium of communication takes the place of print in providing a record of man's culture, of his best ideas and his most penetrating thought, skillful teachers will make use of many types of communication in promoting interest and skill in reading.

The Influence of the Community

The little child is molded by the forces of the community in which he lives, the primary community which is his home, and the secondary community—comprising his playmates, the milkman, the policeman, the mailman, the man at the nearby confectionery store, and the near neighbors. His early attitudes toward race, religion, and minority groups are largely obtained from his community. It may even be a factor in his choice of vocation.

Of marked significance is the impact of the urban community on the attitudes and behavior of youth. The chaotic stimulation, impersonality, and complexity of organization of the city are factors that are easily detrimental to youth. The family in the industrial area faced with problems of housing, of multiple dwelling units, of irregular working hours, and of working mothers all too often fails to provide a security-giving environment. Even the close friendship ties of the immediate neighborhood, which in the smaller community serve as controls in the upbringing of youth, are almost nonexistent in many sections of large cities. People live in the same communities for years without knowing next-door neighbors. They come from hundreds of small towns, since only a few are born and nurtured in these fast-growing industrial areas. They are, quite literally, displaced persons.

The little child is often lost if he strays more than three doors from home. No one knows him. He grows up in a rapid-moving and hostile world. "No children wanted," "No ball playing here," "Keep off the grass," "Danger—Keep out" are but a few indications of his environment. The phenomenon of urbanism may be creating a new kind of personality, one no longer a product of the family and neighborhood, but a product of the urban way of life.

It is little wonder that these pressures often make young people feel unwanted and shoved around. If over long periods of time the young person has few relationships that compensate for these pressures, he tends to base his behavior on codes accepted by juveniles but unacceptable to society generally. When the schools in these communities provide mass methods of instruction, "Grand-Central-Station" type of buildings, and cold and impersonal relationships in classrooms, it is small wonder, as some psychologists suggest, that schools appear to contribute to the maladjustment of youth.

As the school and community shape the child's values and behavior, they influence his attitude toward reading. Teachers and librarians in planning reading guidance programs should understand the community culture and take it into account in building rapport with pupils and planning for their individual needs and interests. Otherwise they cannot expect pupils to regard their book recommendations with favor—or their guidance activities with respect.

Collecting Background Information on Children

These, then, are the screens through which the guidance person must look in understanding the factors that influence the learning and behavior of children and youth and, in turn, their reading. If, in addition, he is able to collect background information on his own pupils, he commands another resource in providing more adequately for their individual needs and abilities. On subsequent pages a number of techniques for gathering background information are described.

Cumulative Records

It has become almost routine procedure for the school staff to collect and organize certain types of information about each child: his birth date, home address, vocations of the parents, his academic record, health record, and the schools he has attended. His scores on learning aptitude tests, and on tests of basic skills and vocational aptitude are usually included. As these records accumulate year by year, they provide a considerable number of vital statistics. Yet these, by themselves, tell little about the child as a unique personality. To be really useful the cumulative record should contain many anecdotes and other types of information as well.

The school librarian cannot be expected to collect these kinds of data on all the pupils in a school. Counselors and homeroom teachers, however, will provide him with the reading scores of pupils and other data that provide useful information about the problems of individual pupils.

Interest Inventories, Personality and Problem Checklists

Inventories, indexes and checklists are useful in collecting information about the child's interests, problems, wishes, hobbies, and reading preferences. There are many available forms that may be recommended for use from grades 1 through 12, and often questionnaires devised by members of the school staff are useful for collecting information desired in a specific situation.

Data collected by the use of these instruments have a twofold value; first, they are invaluable aids in providing knowledge about the wishes, interests, problems, and concerns of the individual pupil. Secondly, the mass data provide pupil reactions to current school programs, majority opinion, and evaluation of the curriculum, thus indicating direction for possible improvement.

For example, if 35 per cent of the children in the fourth, fifth, and sixth grades in a school check reading as the subject they dislike the most, it would seem that teachers responsible for the reading experiences provided pupils in the school might pursue further study to find out why.

It has been the experience of many school staffs that pupils enjoy checking these forms, that it seems to provide them with feelings of achievement and, in some cases, a salutary chance to do a little griping. Pupils, however, need to have complete faith and trust in the adult who administers the instruments. They need to be sure that information they give will not be used against them. Otherwise, they will give only "safe" answers.[19]

Questionnaires can be devised that provide the librarian or teacher invaluable clues to the present status of reading in the school and furnish him guideposts for the selection of appropriate reading materials and reading experiences for youth.

Informal Conferences and Interviews

A talk with a child gives the adult a "perspective of the child's world"—a clue to his behavior. A talk with a child is often worth more than a dozen items in a cumulative record folder.

On the part of the interviewer there needs to be a kind of empathy, a sharing of interests and concerns, a genuine intelligent

[19] Among many reputable study forms are:

Ross L. Mooney, *Problem Check Lists, Junior High School Form and Senior High School Form* (New York: The Psychological Corporation, 1950).

Paul A. Witty and David Kopel, *Diagnostic Child Study Record, Form III, Pupil Report of Interests and Activities* (Evanston, Ill.: Northwestern University Psychological Clinic, 1936).

Arthur T. Jersild and Ruth J. Tasch, *Children's Interests and What They Suggest for Education* (New York: Bureau of Publications, Teachers College, Columbia University, 1949), p. 91

Detroit Public Schools, *Pupil's Inventory Form 8199 and Student's Inventory Form 8898* (Detroit: Board of Education of the City of Detroit, Michigan, 1953).

Gertrude Hildreth, *Personality and Interest Inventory* (New York: Bureau of Publications, Teachers College, Columbia University, 1935).

H. H. Remmers and others, *SRA Junior Inventory* (Chicago: Science Research Associates, 1955).

H. H. Remmers and others, *SRA Youth Inventory* (Chicago: Science Research Associates, 1953).

regard for the worth of the other. Suggestions like the following have been found useful in interviewing:

Wait until the pupil is at ease before asking direct questions. Share your own interests. *Tell* him something first.

Discuss his hobbies, play preferences, leisure activities, his movie and television preferences, his reading.

Inquire about brothers and sisters, jobs he is required to do, his friends.

Put yourself in the child's place. Don't ask him for information you would hesitate to give yourself.

Don't imply the answers to your questions.

Listen to what he says and show interest and approval.

Don't, in any case, express disapproval or shock.

Sociometric Techniques

Information may be obtained about the relationships in a class group with the insertion of two or three friendship questions in an interest inventory. The respondent may be asked (1) to name his very best friend in the group, (2) to name the persons he likes to have as friends, and (3) to name the pupil he might like but doesn't know in his group. Other questions can be devised to fit the particular situation. Tabulation of these data yield scores for the number of choices a child receives, or does not receive. Thus, the teacher discovers the leaders, the isolated and rejected children and the relationships between the cliques and sub-groups comprising his class. Results can be used in planning group and committee work, and particularly is this information of value in guiding the reading of individuals.

Observation

The simplest approach to understanding the child is to observe what he does. Then if the observer makes a record, he has taken another step in one of the most objective methods of studying individual behavior. The value of such a record resides in the fact that it is a statement of what actually happened, rather than an expression of judgment of character traits or behavior exhibited by the child. Even if recording this kind of information is too time-consuming, the skilled observer can learn a great deal about children by listening and watching. He notes posture and dress. Is the child well nourished? relaxed? withdrawn? Does he show bodily aggression? Is he boisterous? cheerful? always alone? It is not difficult to identify symptoms of behavior, but it is a more perplexing problem to understand and treat causes. The skilled guidance person understands the paradox of behavior. He knows that beneath an aggressive, hard-boiled exterior is usually a troubled, insecure child. Listening to children's conversations, observing them in many different situations about the school give valuable leads to their abilities, their interests, and their needs. To an understanding adult there is nothing more stimulating than skillful, objective observance of youth.

Autobiographies and Reading Records

Unless writing is an extremely laborious occupation for the individual, he will pursue with enthusiasm the request for the story of his life. Autobiographies are authentic sources of information about pupils. The person directing the activity may suggest the inclusion of such items as the pupil's family, his leisure interests, his vocational aspirations, his wishes, his concerns, his past experiences, what he likes and dislikes to do. Older pupils may be asked to include in their stories a reading autobiography, and to comment briefly on their favorite books, their earliest recollections about books and reading, their present methods for choosing books, their current reading interests.

Another useful method of understanding the child's reading patterns and the breadth and scope of his interests is the reading record. There are record forms that may be purchased from school supply companies or the school may devise a simple form of its own. Many school libraries use a reading record card which is filed at the circulation desk and on which is listed the title of every book the child withdraws from the library. This, of course, does not give an accurate picture of books actually read. The chief value of any type of reading record is the motivation it provides the individual to extend his reading interests. It should never be used as a basis for marks or other rewards.

SUMMARY AND IMPLICATIONS

Knowing and understanding the factors that influence children is a first important step in guiding and teaching them, and knowing the needs and problems of the individual pupil an essential second step. The skill with which the teacher and librarian collect background information, the penetration with which they generalize about children are crucial factors in guidance. Even if no deliberate program follows, they will treat children more objectively and sympathetically, for "just to understand makes all the difference."

This applies with equal force in reading guidance. Knowledge of the reader and the factors that influence his reading tends to make the teacher or librarian less haphazard in his selection of reading materials, more skillful in planning reading activities. The measure of his success will be in direct proportion to the rapport that exists between him and the pupil and the skill he exhibits in using books not as devices but as a rich ground for guidance.

PROBLEMS FOR DISCUSSION AND STUDY

1. If you were the high school librarian in Elmtown, what would you do to help solve some of the problems of the school and community? (See *Elmtown Youth* in the list of Other Suggested Readings.)

2. Assume that you have collected data from 100 elementary school children by using Jersild's *Interest Finder*. How would you use the data in reading guidance?

3. Examine one of the studies of reading interests listed subsequently in Other Suggested Readings to familiarize yourself with the techniques used. Discuss your findings.

4. What do you consider good reading behavior?

5. Observe, listen to, and talk with two or three children. Ask them about their friends, their pets, their interests and hobbies. Try to see how much information that might help you in guiding their reading you can get about them during ten minutes of casual conversation.

6. Discuss all the factors influencing the reading of boys and girls. Try to rank them in order of their importance.

7. If you are at this time employed as a teacher or as a school librarian, make a survey of a class of boys and girls to ascertain their interests, needs, and problems.

8. Summarize the factors that influence the growth and learning of youth and outline specifically how you will use the information in giving reading guidance to children.

9. Collect and organize information relating to the relative influence of the following factors in determining the reading interests of boys and girls: home background, sex, age, intelligence, other media of communication.

10. Interview three adolescents to discover the influence of the home, school, community, libraries, movies, television, age, sex, and general interests on their reading. Organize and summarize the interviews. Include a list of questions which you used in the interviews.

11. Investigate the present status of communication media in your community as they affect the reading of children and youth.

12. Report in some detail a number of studies on reading interests appearing in recent periodicals. What implications do they suggest for action in improving the reading of youth?

13. How would you attempt to find out about the school-community if you were a recently appointed member of the school staff? You might investigate some recent community studies for possible approaches.

OTHER SUGGESTED READINGS

Adams, Fay. *Educating America's Children.* New York: Ronald Press, 1954.

Baldwin, Alfred L. *Behavior and Development in Childhood.* New York: Dryden Press, 1955.

Baruch, Dorothy. *How to Live With Your Teen-ager.* New York: McGraw-Hill Book Co., 1953.

Burton, William H. *Reading in Child Development.* Indianapolis: Bobbs Merrill, 1956.

Cunningham, Ruth and others. *Understanding Group Behavior of Boys and Girls.* New York: Bureau of Publications, Teachers College, Columbia University, 1951.

Davis, Allison and Havighurst, Robert J. *Father of the Man.* Boston: Houghton Mifflin Co., 1947.

Davis, Allison. *Social-Class Influence Upon Learning.* Cambridge, Mass.: Harvard University Press, 1948.

Frank, Josette. *Your Child's Reading Today.* Garden City, N.Y.: Doubleday & Co., 1954.

Gesell, Arnold L. and Ilg, Francis. *Child Development.* New York: Harper & Brothers, 1949.

Gray, W. S. "Reading." *Encyclopedia of Educational Research.* Edited by Walter Monroe. New York: Macmillan Co., 1950, pp. 965-1005.

Havighurst, Robert J. *Human Development and Education.* New York: Longmans, Green & Co. 1953.

Hollingshead, August De Belmont. *Elmtown Youth.* New York: John Wiley & Sons, 1949.

Hymes, J. L. *Understanding Your Child.* New York: Prentice-Hall, 1952.

Jenkins, Gladys, and others. *These Are Your Children.* Chicago: Scott, Foresman & Co., 1953.

Jersild, Arthur T. and Tasch, Ruth J. *Children's Interests and What They Suggest for Education.* New York: Bureau of Publications, Teachers College, Columbia University, 1949.

Lazar, May. *Reading Interests, Activities and Opportunities of Bright, Average and Dull Children.* New York: Bureau of Publications, Teachers College, Columbia University, 1937.

Mitchell, Lucy (Sprague), ed. *Know Your Children in School.* New York: Macmillan Co., 1954.

National Society for the Study of Education. *Mass Media of Communication.* Fifty-third Yearbook, Part 2. Chicago: Unversity of Chicago Press, 1954.

Norvell, George W. *The Reading Interests of Young People.* Boston: D. C. Heath & Co., 1950.

Olsen, Edward G. and others. *School and Community.* New York: Prentice-Hall, 1954.

Rankin, Marie. *Children's Interest in Library Books of Fiction.* New York: Teachers College, Columbia University, 1944.

Redl, Fritz. *Helping Teachers Study Their Children.* Lansing: Michigan Cooperative Teacher Education Study, 1941.

Stendler, Celia. *Children of Brasstown.* Urbana: University of Illinois, 1949.

Strang, Ruth. *An Introduction to Child Study.* New York: Macmillan Co., 1951.

Traxler, Arthur E. and Townsend, Agatha. *Eight More Years of Research in Reading*. New York: Educational Records Bureau, 1955.

Wertham, Fredric. *Seduction of the Innocent*. New York: Rinehart & Co., 1954.

Witty, Paul. "Children and TV—A Sixth Report." *Elementary English,* XXXII (November 1955), 469-476.

Wollner, Mary H. B. *Children's Voluntary Reading as an Expression of Individuality*. New York: Bureau of Publications, Teachers College, Columbia University, 1949.

CHAPTER 3

SELECTING AND ORGANIZING LEARNING MATERIALS IN THE SCHOOL

The purpose of a liberal education is not merely to impart knowledge; it is to transform personality by transforming minds. But they cannot be transformed by materials that do not speak directly to the human soul.

—NATHAN PUSEY

No other single factor, save that of the teacher, influences more decisively the learning experiences provided youth in our schools than do the materials of instruction. The most carefully planned reading program fails, the most skillful teacher is handicapped if learning materials are not attractive, appropriate, and easily accessible. Appropriate materials, however, will not suffice unless they are skillfully used. The increased understanding about how children learn, and the extension of mass media of communication have focused attention on the need for teachers and librarians alike to possess a high degree of skill in the selection, organization, and utilization of instructional materials.

The evidence is steadily accumulating to indicate that individual differences in ability to learn are not merely differences in rate of learning, but differences in ability to learn various skills and to learn in various situations and from various materials. It is these findings that have convinced school administrators and teachers that major dependence on the single textbook, the supplementary reader, the work book is no longer acceptable; that diverse and varied media of communication must be used to provide for individual differences since each appears to make a unique contribution to the learning process. Filmstrips, for example, focus the eye upon the visual image of subjects. Models show the shape and formation of objects, records and recordings dramatize the spoken message. Motion pictures present a moving panorama of people and places. TV combines the spoken word and the visual object while books and print not only provide the reader with the record of man's heritage and achievements but allow him to proceed at his own rate, to reread and reflect.

The rapid increase in mass media of communication presents another problem. The avalanche of books, pamphlets, pictures, films, filmstrips, tape recordings, radio and television programs create for school staffs an almost overwhelming task of selection, organization, and utilization.

In 1955 book publishers in the United States issued over 12,589 new titles and new editions of which one twelfth were juveniles. Including the publication of reprints, paperbounds, revised editions, and textbooks, book publishing is at present a $650-million-a-year industry in the United States. More than 1,765 English-language newspapers and 7,640 different magazines were published, and this figure does not include the comics that each month sell about 90 million copies.[1] When one contemplates the number of audio-visual materials currently on the market, the outpouring of government documents, the $9 billion outlay made by industry last year in the production and utilization of communication media, one is led to agree with Louis Shores that the "college library of tomorrow may well contain collections that number 20 million volumes with 6,000 miles of shelving and 750,000 catalog drawers."[2]

The number and variety of communication media make libraries and librarians indispensable in the modern school, but the provision of these resources does not solve the problem. Only as the teachers and librarians work together to help pupils become skilled in their use will these media adequately provide for effective learning. This suggests, therefore, that while the school librarian will take over much of the detail involved in processing, organizing, and maintaining instructional materials, teachers need to be equally well acquainted with them in order to help select

[1] "American Book Publication—1955," *Publishers Weekly*, CLXIX (January 2, 1956), 223.

[2] Louis Shores, ed., *Challenges to Librarianship*. (Tallahassee: Florida State University, 1954), p. 5.

them and teach young people to use them effectively. On subsequent pages, procedures are suggested to aid in the selection of both printed and audio-visual materials which comprise the library collection in the modern school.

Is the Book Good?

The person who evaluates and selects children's books considers their literary quality, their appropriateness for the pupils who will use them, and the specific needs and uses to which they may contribute. Three questions provide direction. Is the book good? Is it good for the children in this school? What is it good for? To answer these questions adequately calls for real skill in book evaluation. For the uninitiated the use of rather specific questions serve to identify evaluative criteria.

Criteria for Judging Book Values

Scope and Content:

1. Will the content contribute to the child's understanding and appreciation of the world about him and to his social and emotional adjustment?

2. Does the content fit the needs and interests of the age group for which the book is written?

3. Are the characters worthy of the young person's enthusiasm?

4. Do the incidents seem forced or are they plausible, considering the characters and situations depicted?

5. Does the book give a real picture of life?

Style and Presentation:

1. Is the book well written? Does it have simplicity, vitality, sincerity?

2. Does the plot move simply and directly toward a climax without long descriptions and involved minor plots and characters?

3. Are readability factors controlled? Is it written with clarity?

Physical and Textual Characteristics:

1. Is the size of the book, its shape and illustrations, the size of type appropriate to the contents and to the readers for whom the book is designed?

2. Is the binding durable and attractive?

3. Is the book illustrated? Are the illustrations inviting and intriguing? Do they reflect the child's world, have a story-telling quality?

A number of additional criteria need to be considered in selecting non-fiction books.

Scope and Content:

1. Are the concepts and ideas presented within the understanding of pupils for whom the material is designed?

2. Are the content and subject significant? Is the material a real contribution to the subject? Are the facts and information accurate?

3. Is the treatment of the subject balanced and original?

4. Is the author an authority in the field, or, if not, has his research been objective and comprehensive?

5. Do the copyright and revision dates indicate that the material is up to date?

Style and Presentation:

1. Is the presentation of material interesting, balanced, significant, and appealing?

2. Is the writing smooth, clear, and dynamic?

Physical and Textual Characteristics:

1. Does the book have appropriate illustrative material, such as pictures, graphs, maps, and charts which clarify and contribute to the content?

2. Is the book adequately indexed and illustrated?

3. Are bibliographies up to date and selective?

4. Is the type clear and the form of the book appropriate to the subject and to its readers?

No method of evaluating books is more rewarding to the selector than the direct examination of the book. He skims through the book hurriedly. and makes decisions about its value. He notes the author and publisher. He glances through the preface to assess the author's purpose. He reads the table of contents to discover the scope of the material. He compares the book with others in the same field. He examines the illustrations. Some books he skims and others he reads from cover to cover. He practices ways of reading rapidly. His eyes need not look at every sentence. They can move rapidly down and across the page. Using evaluative criteria, he analyzes and evaluates as he reads.

Yet the best trained and most enthusiastic person cannot spend the time and energy required for reading and evaluating every book at first hand. It is unlikely that book stores are easily accessible to all school communities. Publishers are able to send examination copies only to the large school systems. The majority of teachers and librarians must rely on aids and tools for evaluating and selecting learning materials, and the judicious use of authoritative lists and aids in book selection is recommended as time-saving and efficient. Like any other skill, skill in evaluating books does not come at the first trial. It takes long practice. Individual judgment, therefore, should be augmented. If, however, the teacher and librarian depend on lists exclusively they need to make sure that they use the most authoritative ones.

Aids in Book Selection

The number and variety of book lists, book reviewing magazines, and other aids in book selection make the problem of choice a perplexing one. Schools cannot afford to procure all of them. Choices must be made. One needs to ask: Which are reliable and highly selective, which have been carefully developed by authorities in the field? For what purposes have they been developed? Which are critical in their analysis and evaluation, which merely descriptive?

For example, publishers' lists and reviews should not be relied upon exclusively, even though the company is highly reputable. Publishers' lists are descriptive, produced for the purpose of selling. On the other hand, there are many authoritative lists and bibliographies so carefully developed that the inclusion of a title in the list is a sufficient recommendation.

Among basic lists that can be used with considerable confidence are those issued under the imprint of the Bowker Company and the H. W. Wilson Company; those developed by professional organizations, such as the American Library Association, the Association for Childhood Education International, and the National Council of Teachers of English; those prepared by state departments of education and by many school and public library systems. Considerable dependence can be placed on reviews and lists that appear in standard library publications, general educational periodicals, and a few newspapers that have special book reviewing sections devoted to children's books, such as the New York *Times*, the New York *Herald Tribune* and the *Christian Science Monitor*.

The following titles are suggested as indispensable aids in book selection that should be available in all schools.

A Basic Book Collection for Elementary Grades. Compiled by a subcommittee of the American Library Association Editorial Committee. 6th ed. Chicago: American Library Association, 1956, $2.00.

Describes and evaluates over 1,000 books for children. A classified, annotated list with fiction, picture, and easy books listed separately and grade levels suggested, kindergarten through eight. Full buying information, subject headings, and Wilson card data given under each title. A magazine list, and an author, title, and subject index are included.

Basic Book Collection for Junior High Schools. Compiled by a subcommittee of the American Library Association Editorial Committee. 2d ed. Chicago: American Library Association, 1956, $1.75.

A classified, annotated list similar in organization to the *Basic Book Collection for Elementary Grades*, selected with the assistance of an advisory committee of teachers and librarians expressly for junior high school pupils. About 600 titles are listed.

Full buying information and subject headings are given. A list of magazines and an author, title, and subject index are included.

A Basic Book Collection for High Schools. Compiled by a subcommittee of the American Library Association Editorial Committee, Mariana Kennedy McAllister, Chairman; with the assistance of consultants from the National Education Association, National Council of Teachers of English, National Council for the Social Studies, and Association for Supervision and Curriculum Development. 6th ed. Chicago: American Library Association, 1957, $2.75.

A selective list of about 1,500 books in the high school field. It is arranged by Dewey Classification number. Annotations for each title, including some indication of reading level when relevant. Suggested subject headings, Wilson card data, Library of Congress card numbers, and full buying information are given for each title. A list of magazines for high schools, selection aids for audio-visual materials, and a list of publishers are included.

The Book List and Subscription Books Bulletin. Chicago: American Library Association, $6.00. Published twice monthly, once in August.

A selective, classified, and annotated guide to current books. The sections devoted to Children's Books, Books for Young People, and Free and Inexpensive Materials are invaluable to teachers and school librarians. Full buying, cataloging, and classification information is given for each book, and grade and interest level are indicated. Other features include lists of new editions and government publications. Library of Congress numbers and the availability of Wilson cards are indicated. Beginning September 1, 1956, the *Subscription Books Bulletin* became a part of the new *Book List.* Formerly issued as a quarterly by the American Library Association, the *Bulletin* gives unbiased critical reviews of encyclopedias, dictionaries, and sets of reference books of a general nature sold by the subscription method. The "recommended" or "not recommended" closing statements in the reviews are invaluable to schools which must evaluate and select books on a subscription basis. There has been no change in the reviews or procedures in the combined publication.

Bulletin of the Children's Book Center. Chicago: University of Chicago Library, $2.50 a year. Published monthly except August.

A critical guide to books for children and young people. Books are carefully and critically evaluated wth emphasis on developmental values. Full buying information is included for each title and grade levels are suggested.

Buying List of Books for Small Libraries. Compiled by Orilla Thompson Blackshear. 8th ed. Chicago: American Library Association, 1954.

A basic classified list containing approximately 1,800 titles suggested for first purchase in the small public library. The sections devoted to *Young People's Books, Children's Books* and *Sources of Free and Inexpensive Materials* are of special value to the school librarian and teacher. Gives complete buying information, classification number and descriptive annotations. L.C. numbers and Wilson card availability are included.

Children's Catalog. Compiled by Marion L. McConnell and Dorothy Herbert West. 9th ed. New York: H. W. Wilson Co., 1956.

Listing over 3,200 children's books recommended for school and public libraries by a group of experienced librarians and specialists in children's literature, the catalog is an essential aid in book selection for both elementary and junior high schools. Part I is a classified catalog giving annotations, descriptive notes, and full cataloging information for each book. Appropriate grade levels are noted. Books especially recommended by the consultants are starred and double starred. Part II is an author, title, subject, and analytical index in dictionary form with entries for authors, illustrators, editors, and compilers, as well as subject and title entries. Fairy tales are entered in the analytical index under individual titles. Wilson cards are available for all listed titles published since 1938. A graded list of titles and a publishers' directory are included. Sold on the service basis with supplements.

Horn Book Magazine. Boston: Horn Book, $4.00 a year. Published bi-monthly.

Each issue contains selected lists of books and reading for children and young people, and also occasional lists for high school and current adult books. Well written articles about authors, illustrators, and books.

Library Journal. New York: R. R. Bowker Co., $7.00 a year. Published twice monthly September through June, monthly in July and August. Includes *Junior Libraries,* which may be purchased by schools separately for $3.75, September through May.

The book lists, articles and reviews make this periodical useful to both teachers and librarians. Contains excellent annotations of books for the youngest through high school grades, also lists of films and recordings. The lists of *Starred Books from the Library Journal* are issued from time to time as reprints.

Standard Catalog for High School Libraries. Edited by Dorothy Herbert West and Marion L. McConnell. 7th ed. New York: H. W. Wilson Co., 1957.

Lists 3,585 books for use in both junior and senior high schools, of which 766 are single starred, and 372 are double starred, indicating especial recommendations. Part I consists of a classified annotated catalog giving for each book full cataloging information including Library of Congress card numbers and availability of Wilson printed catalog cards. Additional titles for possible purchase are noted at end of the classes. Part II is an author, title, subject, and analytical index in dictionary form. Part III lists the publishers represented in the Catalog. Sold on the service basis.

Standard Catalog for High School Libraries, with Catholic Supplement. Edited by Dorothy Herbert West and Marion L. McConnell. 7th ed. New York: H. W. Wilson Co., 1957.

Includes all the material in the regular edition with the addition of a list of 643 titles in the fields of Catholic history, biography, literature, and religion. The supplement is not available separately.

Wilson Library Bulletin. New York: H. W. Wilson Co. $3.00 a year. Published monthly, except July and August.

This publication presents a "practical approach to all phases of librarianship." Special departments such as Current Reference Books, School and Children's Libraries, and Displays for the Month provide information useful to teachers and librarians.

Is the Book Good for These Children?

Reading authorities, literary critics, and book publishers agree that children's books should not only be good, but they should be good for children. Increasingly they disagree about who is to judge what is good for children and what criteria of selection should receive major emphasis.

In the past heavy emphasis has been given to the literary quality of the book and to the lure of "distinguished literature." Many authorities assume that when children are exposed to books of the finest quality, they will acquire appreciation and love for literature, since it follows that "great literature meets the needs and interests of the child." People holding this viewpoint accept nothing but "the best" in literature for children, and there is some evidence to defend their position.

No adult who has experienced the breathless silence that prevails when children listen to stories that have stood the test of time will question the appeal and allure of great literature. Books like *Tom Sawyer* and *Little Women* are beloved by children primarily because Tom, Jo, Meg, Beth, and Amy are real children, as true to life in the 1950's as they were half a century ago. They speak to all children, and today these books continue to head the lists of children's favorites. Other children's classics do not fare as well, however, and it is the considered judgment of many educators that books for children must stand the test of the child's approval.

The findings of many reading studies indicate that it may be unrealistic to select books without giving major consideration to the culture patterns, motivations, problems, and needs of the particular children for whom the books are selected; that a book may satisfy every literary test, may receive the enthusiastic acclaim of adults, may appear on all the authoritative lists, may be a real contribution to literature, and yet find little approval from more than a few exceptional youthful readers.

Marie Rankin, in her study of children's interests, found that few of the Newbery award books stood high in popularity, while a number of them appear to be genuinely disliked by young readers.[3] George Norvell found that over half of the selections read in high school literature classes were actively disliked by pupils.[4] It can be assumed that the selections were of excellent literary quality. According to May Hill Arbuthnot books selected for children must be liked by children. She states:

> Children have always had the skill to dodge what bores them, and ever since printing began we have seen them reaching around and across obtuse adults for such reading matter as they wished.[5]

And she cites Paul Hazard as giving them credit for resisting dull books that adults try to inflict upon them.[6]

Somewhere between the two extreme viewpoints would appear to be a reasonable stand for the book selector. With careful consideration of the lure of the beautifully written book and with painstaking analysis of the cultural backgrounds, the interests, activities, concerns, and motivations of the pupils in a given school, teachers and librarians should be able to select books of high quality that an overwhelming majority of the children in the school will like because the books, first of all, meet individual needs and abilities.

For example, the person selecting books and other materials for primary school children will be guided by what has been learned about the interests of little chidren. He will select animal stories that involve personification, folk tales, and realistic stories of everyday experiences of small boys and girls. If the school happens to be in a rural community, the selector will recognize also the pupils' special interests and may select a disproportionate number of picture books and easy books that tell of farms and tractors and farm animals.

Teachers and librarians in communities where a great majority of the children come from homes of depressed socio-

---

[3] Marie Rankin, *Children's Interest in Library Books of Fiction* (New York: Bureau of Publications, Teachers College, Columbia University, 1941).

[4] George Norvell, *Reading Interests of Young People* (Boston: D. C. Heath, & Co., 1950).

[5] May Hill Arbuthnot, *Children and Books* (Chicago: Scott, Foresman & Co., 1957), p. 15.

[6] Paul Hazard, *Books, Children and Men* (Boston: Horn Book, 1947), p. 47-49.

economic status, where books and reading are quite foreign to the existing cultural patterns in the home, will take into account the reading choices of the average child as they select books for a school. In addition, they will keep in mind a number of other factors that influence the reading of these children, such as lack of regard for reading in the home, lack of readiness to read, and deficiency in reading skill. Where this situation prevails a school staff will need to select a disproportionate number of books of high interest and easy vocabulary.

The continuing problem of retardation in reading creates or indicates other problems in the selection of appropriate materials. During the last decade increased attention has been given to readability factors in books for children. Publishers of textbooks employ reading experts who proctor vocabulary to safeguard readability. Sentence structure is examined. Are the sentences long? Do they contain several phrases or clauses? Such painstaking analysis, however, sometimes produces a book with a style and vocabulary that resemble pablum, "tasteless but nourishing."

To place too much dependence on readability factors is unwise, particularly when discrepancies appear in the results obtained when the same book is checked for reading difficulty with several of the existing readability formulae. Teresa Klein checked twenty-five children's books with the three formulae developed by Flesch, Lorge, and Witty. She found considerable variation in results, and wide discrepancy between the grade level suggested in authoritative lists of children's books and the grade levels obtained by using the various formulae.[7]

The problem of reading difficulty and reading retardation is a serious one, and there are few teachers who would not agree that every attempt should be made to provide materials to fit individual abilities. However, in the considered judgment of many authorities, the aspect of high interest is more significant than vocabulary difficulty. If a child's interest in a subject is intense, he will read material which is far beyond his reading level.

[7] Teresa Klein, "Using Readability Formulae in Selecting Books" (Unpublished master's thesis, State University Teachers College, Geneseo, New York, 1953).

The little child who reads the Beatrix Potter books is not bothered by such phrases as "eating too much lettuce is soporific." He gets the idea, even though he may not understand all the words. To question the value of the Beatrix Potter books because they do not stand scientific readability tests pin-points the danger of using any single evaluative criterion in selecting books. From available evidence, it seems fair to assume that books should be selected with deliberate consideration of a number of factors, one of which is the needs of a unique group of children. It is unrealistic to expect that the same collection of books, no matter how excellent the quality, will be appropriate for all school populations.

What Is the Book Good For?

Emerson's statement, "Be not simply good, be good for something," may be considered a tiresome commonplace, yet it is a useful adage when applied to books. In making choices among the hundreds of available juvenile titles the selector must consider their utilitarian value. In selecting non-fiction books he asks: Will the book provide information in science or art? Will it answer the kinds of questions the children in this school ask? Does it relate to their interests and hobbies? Will it provide insight and knowledge about problems and subjects discussed in the classroom? Will it provide specialized information for gifted children?

While the uses of the book have always been paramount in the selection of non-fiction titles, recently fiction has been evaluated in terms of its usefulness in the curriculum. Social studies teachers choose fiction titles that give a picture of American life, that reflect the social problems of our times, that sensitize youth to the needs and problems of others. Reading lists appearing in curriculum guides and in resource units on transportation, communication, food, and shelter—to mention only a few—include fiction titles, picture books, biography, poetry, and folklore as well as books of information. Current bibliographies in science include books of information, biographies of scientists, and science fiction.

Findings from studies in intergroup education, mental health, and citizenship education have indicated values in the use of fiction titles for teaching democratic beliefs and skill in human relationships. Emphasis on using books to help youth with their developmental tasks has created teacher awareness of the need to select books with due attention to their uses.

Is the book good? Is it good for the children of this school? What, specifically, is it good for? These three questions place heavy responsibility on the book selector. To answer them adequately means that he must know books in terms of their quality and accessibility. It means that he must understand children and what they want and look for in books. It suggests that he know the school curriculum and the values in books.

Building a Book Collection

Although it takes real skill to select single titles for purchase, it requires a variety of skills to build a well balanced and adequate book collection for a school. To be completely convinced of this fact one needs only to visit a number of schools where library collections have been developed without the services of a librarian. The observer usually encounters large numbers of inappropriate, dilapidated, obsolete books. Rarely is the collection balanced, well organized or attractively displayed.

What are the steps to be taken in developing an adequate book collection in a school?

1. *An evaluation of the present collection should be made.* In judging the adequacy of a book collection the following questions are useful: Are all curriculum fields adequately represented? Are reference books up to date, authoritative, and appropriate? Have all obsolete and worn-out books been discarded? Are from 25 to 40 per cent of the volumes in the collection added copies? Is the collection suited to the needs, interests, and abilities of the school population that uses the library? The entire collection

needs to be checked against authoritative lists for adequacy, appropriateness, and balance.

2. *Book selection should be a daily undertaking.* The school librarian or the book selector will expedite the process of book selection if he keeps a record day by day of such items as the following: requests for books that cannot be furnished; reference questions that cannot be adequately answered; notations about books lost or discarded that should be replaced; notes and notices of new books that have been recommended by teachers and pupils; titles of books seen in displays or reviewed and included in approved lists. All of these he will note on "p" slips and file. When it is time to send in a book order, he has fairly good record of book needs and a basic list of titles on which to start building a balanced book order.

3. *Order routines should be planned and followed consistently.* On the "p" slips kept throughout the year the librarian, as he finds time, should fill in the title, author, publisher, edition, copyright date, and price, and the number of copies required. Decisions need to be made about how books are to be purchased—whether from a jobber, a local book store, or directly from the publisher. In dealing with a jobber only one book order is required and usually discounts are favorable. However, the school administrator should share in this decision.

When the order has been carefully analyzed, evaluated, and approved by the school administrator, an alphabetical list should be typed from the cards. This list becomes the official book order. The original order cards should be saved and marked as "outstanding orders." The date on which the book was ordered should be noted on them and when books are received this date should likewise be placed on the card as a purchase record. Routines may vary from school to school and the librarian or teacher follows any special order procedure required by the school.

4. *Efforts should be made to acquire an adequate collection.* Few schools have adequate funds for the purchase of books and instructional materials. Many school systems are extremely gen-

erous in textbook allowances and far less so in providing funds for library materials. This occurs when boards of education are not given adequate information as to the needs and uses of the library collection.

Requests for funds should be accompanied by information on existing standards for book budgets recommended by school accrediting agencies. The librarian may use the standards suggested by the American Association of School Librarians of $1.50 per pupil yearly for the purchase of library books, periodicals, and other printed materials, and in addition special funds every two or three years for the purchase of encyclopedias. This sum includes bindery costs as well. Other accrediting agencies suggest a slightly lower figure, ranging from 75c to $1.00 per pupil with a suggested ratio of five books per pupil.

Another method that the librarian may use to stretch the budget is to use reprints, rebinds, and inexpensive editions of books. Among a number of available buying lists of inexpensive books is one developed by Catherine Adamson,[8] for elementary schools, in which 700 titles at prices less than $1.50 are listed. The Association for Childhood Education International has also developed lists of inexpensive books. The Cadmus reprints published and sold by E. M. Hale & Co. and sold only to schools and libraries are worth investigating. This list includes a wide variety of titles at reasonable prices. The books are printed from original plates, and the binding is unusually sturdy.

Many publishers also publish school editions printed on strong paper with reinforced bindings. They use the same illustrations as for their trade editions. Often these books are inexpensive and durable. Many librarians order reinforced bindings on books that receive hard use. Although these bindings increase the original cost of the book, they are a money-saving device because of the extra life of the book.

After the librarian or teacher-librarian knows what funds he will have for books, he should place one large order a year

[8] Catherine Adamson, *Inexpensive Books for Girls and Boys* (3d ed. Chicago: American Library Association, 1952).

and keep an appropriate fund for emergency purchase and for small orders to insure a steady flow of new books to display cases and library shelves the year round.

5. *The collection must be organized for service.* The story is only half told when the books are selected, purchased, and delivered to the school. They must then be processed, classified, cataloged, and shelved. Time and motion studies reveal that it requires at least an hour for the skilled librarian to process each new book for circulation. With high regard for the good will of mother-librarians, members of PTA organizations, principals, and teachers who attempt to organize book collections, an evaluation of their contribution leads one to conclude that it is wasteful unless they acquire the necessary skills. In schools too small to employ librarians or teacher-librarians, teachers and principals can depend on authoritative lists and other book selection sources. In organizing their book collections they will need to follow procedures outlined in manuals and books on library organization and administration. It should be pointed out, however, that the organization of the collection, no matter how small the school, should be in the hands of a trained librarian. The use of printed catalog cards is an important time-saving device for the school librarian. This service may be obtained from the Library of Congress or the H. W. Wilson Company, with the Wilson cards particularly appropriate and useful for the average school library.

Selecting and Organizing Non-Book Materials

Although books comprise the foundation of the library, our rapidly changing world calls for the use of all kinds of current materials to report the swift progress in science, politics and the arts. In many high schools there is some anxiety on the part of teachers and librarians about the selection of current non-book materials, particularly those printed materials dealing with controversial subjects. The American Library Association and the American Association of School Librarians have acted to safeguard the right of youth to explore and examine both sides of controversial subjects under proper and skillful guidance. Even so, school staffs recognize their own responsibility, and seek dependable criteria for the selection of current materials. Many of the criteria that apply to books are equally valid in selecting non-book materials. Other sources and aids for selection are summarized on succeeding pages.

Choosing Magazines

There is slight need to indicate the tremendous appeal of magazines for children and youth. With the advent of the picture magazine which makes reading relatively unnecessary, with the publication of magazines that present on-the-spot news, that interpret current life and times, and the arts and sciences, it is small wonder that boys and girls are avid readers of magazines, and that authorities suggest the expenditure of from 10 to 15 per cent of the school's book budget for their purchase.

Not many magazines are published exclusively for younger children, possibly because the potential reader so soon wants to read adult magazines, possibly because present-day juvenile magazines no longer appear to hold the individual appeal for the younger child that *Youth's Companion* and *St. Nicholas* had for his grandparents.

The librarian or the teacher who selects periodicals for school use needs to consider the curriculum of the school, the age, abilities, interests, and hobbies of the pupils, and the requests of teachers. The magazine must stand the test of good taste and excellent quality in content and format. The use of lists appearing in authoritative sources [9] is recommended. Time and money are often saved if the order is placed with a reputable magazine jobber.

[9] For lists of periodicals suitable for school use consult such sources as:

A Basic Book Collection for High Schools (6th ed. Chicago: American Library Association, 1957).

Laura K. Martin, *Magazines for School Libraries* (Rev. ed. New York: H. W. Wilson Co., 1950).

Periodicals for Small and Medium Sized Libraries (8th ed. Chicago: American Library Association, 1948).

Selecting Newspapers

Three different types of newspapers should be available in schools: the current events papers published exclusively for school use, a local newspaper, and one representing outstanding journalism. There are a number of excellent current events papers published exclusively for the use of pupils in elementary and high schools, and information about them may be found in educational periodicals. These papers should be purchased in quantity so that each pupil has his own to read and discuss as "current events."

As a source of information about the community, a reputable local newspaper should be available, as well as other newspapers that represent outstanding journalism on a national level. When several are chosen, care should be taken to see that they represent a variety of viewpoints.

Important articles and news reports should be clipped and the source and date noted. They should be classified by subject and organized with other vertical file materials in the school library where they can be circulated for classroom use.

Selecting Free and Inexpensive Printed Materials

Useful in conjunction with newspapers and magazines is a wealth of other contemporary materials. Pamphlets, manuals, government documents, graphs, charts, catalogs, travel folders, brochures, bulletins, and official publications of government and industry come off the press in a steady flow. Many of them are extremely valuable, yet they constitute a problem of selection and organization which must be solved. Otherwise they are inaccessible and worthless.

Teachers and librarians both need to assume responsibility for the selection of these materials. There is a tendency to collect too much simply because the materials are inexpensive or free. Standards for selection ought to be rigidly maintained. Larger schools may find it wise to subscribe to the *Vertical File Index* [10] as a source of information about pamphlets. This is a monthly

---

[10] *Vertical File Index;* a subject and title index to selected pamphlet material, monthly (New York: H. W. Wilson Co.), $6.00 a year.

publication, which lists material by subject and includes under each entry descriptive notes, prices, and sources for obtaining the material. The American Library Association *Booklist* [11] also lists free and inexpensive materials and several other lists [12] are dependable sources for both pamphlets and pictures.

The task of ordering and processing these materials is time-consuming. Yet they must all be classified by subject and placed in pamphlet and clipping files, and a simple method of circulation devised for their utilization. Because their value is current and ephemeral by nature, at the end of each school year these files need to be weeded out and much of the material discarded.

CHOOSING AND ORGANIZING AUDIO-VISUAL MATERIALS

Although audio-visual materials can hardly be classified as reading material, they have become a legitimate and valuable part of the instructional materials usually housed in the modern school library. Louis Shores defines audio-visual materials as all media of communication other than the printed word and classifies them in the following categories: community resources including private and public agencies; graphics, including photographs, pictures, posters, and models; projected materials, including recordings, radio programs, and television programs. [13]

The task of selecting and organizing these materials calls for real skill on the part of a school staff. It calls for special furniture and equipment to house adequately the films, filmstrips,

[11] *The Book List and Subscription Books Bulletin;* a guide to current books (Chicago: American Library Association), $6.00 a year.

[12] Other useful sources are:

Bruce Miller, *Free and Inexpensive Teaching Aids* (Riverside, Calif., The Author, 1953).

Elementary Teacher's Guide to Free Curriculum Materials; annual (Randolph, Wis.: Educators Progress Service, 1955).

Free and Inexpensive Learning Materials (7th ed. Nashville, Tenn.: Division of Surveys and Field Services, George Peabody College for Teachers, 1956).

List of Outstanding Curriculum Materials 1951-1954 (1955 ed. Washington, D.C.: Association for Supervision and Curriculum Development, 1955).

Sources of Free and Inexpensive Educational Materials (Chicago: Field Enterprises, 1955).

[13] Louis Shores, *Basic Reference Sources* (Chicago: American Library Association, 1954).

records, posters, projectors, film catalogs. It calls for careful cataloging of these materials so that teachers and pupils alike can go to card files and locate these materials by author, title, or subject exactly as they would locate a book. It calls for the careful selection, organization, and labeling of materials so they can be found quickly.

In too many schools these materials are crowded into cupboards in various rooms in the school, damaged by dust and quite inaccessible. In the very large schools the audio-visual materials are often in the charge of a specially trained person, and are housed in quarters separate from the library. The advantage of keeping all the tools of learning together where a central catalog can be maintained is self-evident. However, if the librarian is to be responsible for the organization and maintenance of these collections, he must be provided with clerical assistance.

Many schools depend on rental services for obtaining films. The price of films makes ownership prohibitive in most schools. This is not true with filmstrips. A school staff can build its own filmstrip library with a relatively small expenditure of funds. In selecting films or filmstrips it is highly important to use authoritative lists and sources in selection. A number of guides, catalogs, indexes, and sources [14] need to be purchased and made available to the teacher in the school. Some of them are issued frequently, which means that the school staff can be informed of new audio-visual materials as they are issued.

Films are usually housed in built-in cupboards with a slot for each film, filmstrips in shallow drawers. They are cataloged much as books are cataloged with the librarian making necessary

[14] Among a number of available sources are:

Educational Film Guide (11th ed. New York: H. W. Wilson Co., 1953), with Supplement service. (Prices on request.)

Educators Guide to Free Films, annual (Randolph, Wis.: Educators Progress Service), $6.00.

Educators Guide to Free Slidefilms (7th ed. Randolph, Wis.: Educators Progress Service, 1955), $5.00.

Educators Guide to Free Tapes, Scripts and Transcriptions (2d ed. Randolph, Wis.: Educators Progress Service, 1956), $4.75.

Filmstrip Guide (3d ed. New York: H. W. Wilson Co., 1954), with Supplement service. (Prices on request.)

Bruce Miller, *Sources of Free Pictures* (1953 ed. Riverside, Calif.: The Author, 1953).

adaptations. Filmstrips may be classified by Dewey Classification or may be indexed and arranged by subject. Colored cards are ordinarily used if they are filed in the regular card catalog, with the title card the main entry.

Models, records, recordings, and flat pictures need to be collected and organized for use. Record catalogs and lists appearing in book reviewing periodicals and educational magazines are dependable sources in selecting records. Flat pictures, including post cards, photographs, and illustrations of all kinds are inexpensive to acquire and convenient to use on bulletin boards and in opaque projectors. A useful collection of pictures can be built with little expense since current magazines may be the chief source of supply. Subject headings need to be assigned to each picture and the pictures filed along with pamphlets and other ephemeral materials.[15]

In administering audio-visual materials the librarian or teacher in charge assumes the following duties: knows sources and selects materials; sees that equipment is kept in repair; trains a student staff to operate the equipment; catalogs materials; arranges a charging system and encourages the use of it.

Audio-visual materials should never be considered competitive with reading. When intelligently used, they arouse curiosity, dramatize and motivate learning. They encourage and give concreteness to many kinds of reading activities.

SUMMARY AND RECOMMENDATIONS

On preceding pages an attempt was made to suggest how the tools of learning are selected and organized. On these tools depends to a considerable degree the learning achievement of children and youth in our schools.

As a result of the increasing demands of the curriculum, school libraries have changed from highly selected book collections to materials centers where all media of communication are

[15] One of the most useful sources of information about the collection and arrangement of audio-visual materials is Margaret I. Rufsvold's *Audio-Visual School Library Service* (Chicago: American Library Association, 1949).

organized, maintained, and circulated for use in the school. In addition, the modern school library houses professional books, resource units, and curriculum guides. Thus it becomes in a very real sense the teaching-learning center of the school, and teachers as well as librarians need to be expert in the selection and use of its resources and facilities.

The reading program is irrevocably dependent on these materials. Teachers and librarians alike need to teach children to be skillful users of the world of communication media of which the printed word "still appears to be the most efficient and effective" method of conveying thought!

When these tools are available and accessible, a school staff can proceed to plan reading programs and organize learning experiences that are meaningful and useful to children and youth.

PROBLEMS FOR DISCUSSION AND STUDY

1. Chandos Reid, in a paper published in the *Wilson Library Bulletin,* May 1951, wrote as follows:

The materials of instruction are then, in every way, the pivot, the center, even the major control of the actual curriculum itself.

What are the implications of this statement for the teacher? For the school librarian?

2. What are the implications of recent developments in curriculum building for the selection and organization of instructional materials?

3. What is the role of the librarian and the teacher in selecting instructional materials?

4. What are the essential steps in selecting books and other materials of instruction for a school?

5. Set up a proposed program for purchasing books and other materials of instruction for a school.

6. Explore and outline the advantages and disadvantages of maintaining the school library as a materials center, housing both printed and audio-visual materials and equipment.

7. Many high schools are presently employing a resource teacher whose entire time is devoted to helping other teachers with instructional materials. On what assumptions is this person employed? What might be the advantages of employing a second librarian instead?

8. Begin to develop a picture file by collecting pictures in available magazines. Work out a simple scheme for classifying them and arranging them by subject.

9. Choose a subject of interest to you. Using a number of sources collect some free and inexpensive materials on the subject.

10. Make a collection of booklists and descriptive materials issued by publishers that would be helpful in selecting books for purchase.

OTHER SUGGESTED READINGS

Adams, Bess Porter. *About Books and Children.* New York: Henry Holt & Co., 1953.

Arbuthnot, May Hill. *Children and Books.* rev. ed. Chicago: Scott Foresman & Co., 1957.

Association for Supervision and Curriculum Development. *Curriculum Materials for Creative Thinking, Living, Teaching.* Washington: The Association, 1956.

Association for Supervision and Curriculum Development. *Using Free Materials in the Classroom.* Washington, D.C.: The Association, 1955.

Children's Book Council. *The World of Children's Books.* New York: Children's Book Council, 1952.

Colby, Jean P. *The Children's Book Field.* New York: Pellegrini and Cudahy, 1952.

Cundiff, Ruby E. *Manual of Techniques in Library Organization.* New York: Wilcox and Follett Co., 1953.

Dean, Howard H. *Effective Communication.* New York: Prentice-Hall, 1953.

Duff, Annis. *Bequest of Wings.* New York: Viking Press, 1944.

East, Marjorie. *Display for Learning.* New York: Dryden Press, 1952.

Eaton, Anne Thaxter. *Reading with Children.* New York: Viking Press, 1947.

Eaton, Anne Thaxter. *Treasure for the Taking.* rev. ed. New York: Viking Press, 1957.

Fenner, Phyllis. *The Proof of the Pudding.* New York: John Day Co., 1957.

Frank, Josette. *Your Child's Reading Today.* Garden City, N.Y.: Doubleday & Co., 1954.

Gardiner, Jewel and Baisden, Leo. *Administering Library Service in the Elementary School.* Chicago, American Library Association, 1954.

Haines, Helen E. *Living with Books.* New York: Columbia University Press, 1950.

Hass, Kenneth B. and others. *Preparation and Use of Audio-Visual Aids.* New York: Prentice-Hall, 1955.

Hazard, Paul. *Books, Children and Men.* Boston: Horn Book, 1947.

Heaps, Willard A. *Book Selection for Secondary School Libraries.* New York: H. W. Wilson Co., 1942.

Ireland, Norma. *The Pamphlet File in School, College, and Public Libraries.* Boston: F. W. Faxon Co., 1954.

Ireland, Norma. *The Picture File in School, College and Public Libraries.* Boston: F. W. Faxon Co., 1952.

Kenworthy, Leonard S. *Introducing Children to the World in Elementary and Junior High Schools.* New York: Harper & Brothers, 1956.

Kinney, Lucien and Dresden, Katherine. *Better Learning Through Current Materials.* Stanford, Calif.: Stanford University Press, 1952.

Logasa, Hannah. *Book Selection Handbook.* Boston: F. W. Faxon Co., 1953.

Martin, Laura K. *Magazines for School Libraries.* New York: H. W. Wilson Co., 1950.

Meigs, Cornelia L. and others. *A Critical History of Children's Literature.* New York: Macmillan Co., 1953.

Miller, Bertha E. (Mahony) and others, comps. *Illustrators of Children's Books.* Boston: Horn Book, 1947.

Miller, Bruce. *So You Want to Start a Picture File.* Riverside, Calif.: The Author, 1952.

Rufsvold, Margaret I. *Audio-Visual School Library Service.* Chicago: American Library Association, 1949.

Smith, Lillian. *The Unreluctant Years.* Chicago: American Library Association, 1953.

Walker, Elinor, ed. *Book Bait; Detailed Notes on Adult Books Popular with Young People.* Chicago: American Library Association, 1957.

Wittich, W. A., and Schuller, C. F. *Audio-Visual Materials.* New York: Harper & Brothers, 1953.

CHAPTER 4

ORGANIZING READING GUIDANCE PROGRAMS

As members of a school staff begin to know and understand children, as they alter the means used to promote more effective guidance, they tend to evaluate and revise the organization and schedule and ultimately to change many of the curriculum experiences provided for pupils.

—ARNOLD R. MEIER

Until recently many teachers have not been greatly concerned about the school's reading program. In the high school, particularly, reading has been regarded as the primary responsibility of teachers of English and the school librarian. Special teachers in the elementary school have tended to consider it the task of the homeroom teacher.

This is no longer true. As school staffs the country over have engaged in programs of curriculum study and development, they have come to understand more clearly the indispensable role of reading in the education of youth, and their own constant and continuing responsibility for it. In turn, this has led to a broadened concept of instruction and guidance in reading and in the skillful use of reading and learning materials.

To develop a school-wide program in reading, kindergarten through high school, requires cooperative planning on the part of every member of the school staff. It calls for some agreements on general objectives. It demands schedules and organization, a way of working, in which all the faculty participate. It requires facilities, including a well equipped, well organized library, and the services of a school librarian.

It is not the purpose of this chapter to discuss and describe every phase of a developmental reading program for a school.

Central in the present discussion is the idea that the child who
cannot and does not read is severely handicapped in learning,
and hence the extension of skill and interest in reading is of paramount importance. There should be no assumption that a blueprint can be given a school staff to follow step by step. Teachers
must tailor a flexible organization to meet their own needs. Some
general guides can be given, however, that suggest a way of working, an orderly procedure for a school staff which is attempting
to improve its reading guidance programs. They are as follows:
evaluating present programs; formulating objectives; providing
facilities; scheduling reading activities; and planning and working cooperatively.

Evaluating the Present Reading Program

Assessing the present state of affairs is an appropriate way
for a school staff to start planning for the improvement of its
reading program since data may provide direction in planning as
well as motivation for an all-out effort. At least an evaluation
of current programs usually dispels complacency and suggests
that improvement is desirable.

Each individual on a school staff engages in a good deal of
informal stock taking as he provides reading experiences for his
pupils. He reflects on questions like the following: Are my pupils
growing in their ability to read with understanding? Are they
using the tools of learning effectively? Are they gaining in their
appreciation of books? Do they like to read? How much and how
well are they now reading? And these same questions will serve
well in a school-wide evaluation of the reading program.

It is not a difficult task to obtain mass data about the effectiveness of the school's reading program. Test instruments and
study forms designed to evaluate reading skills are available
from many sources and today most schools have well organized
testing programs to chart pupil progress. There are, in addition,

many useful instruments that are designed to measure the abilities involved in critical thinking and work-study skills.[1]

Pupil reaction to the reading program can be obtained through the use of questionnaires, if items are skillfully chosen and the pupils made psychologically comfortable in giving information. Questions can be formulated to elicit information about how much pupils read, what and why they read, why they like certain books and dislike others, and how they react to techniques and activities pursued by teachers and librarians.

Although not primarily designed for obtaining information about the effectiveness of the reading program, interest inventories and problem check lists often provide valid data. In one school in which the *Problem Check List*[2] was used, 35 per cent of the pupils checked the problem *trouble with reading*. In another elementary school, where Jersild's *Interest Finder*[3] was given, 45 per cent of the pupils listed reading as the subject "they didn't care about in school." In both schools, these data served a valuable purpose in that they tended to destroy complacency and inertia among teachers and motivated more careful analysis and study of current reading programs. Another valuable source of data about the amount and kind of reading done by pupils is the record of library circulation.

A word of caution may be suggested. Often the use of test data is circumscribed and limited by the inability of staff members to examine findings without defensiveness. Among some teachers the idea is prevalent that any attempt to question present programs and practices in the school is an act of professional disloyalty.

An example of the insecurity of a school staff in handling data is the experience of a high school librarian who sought to discover how his pupils selected their books, and how well they

---

[1] A list of a number of test instruments may be found on p. 206.

[2] Ross L. Mooney, *Problem Check Lists, Junior High School Form* and *Senior High School Form* (New York: Psychological Corporation, 1950).

[3] Arthur T. Jersild and Ruth J. Tasch, *Children's Interests and What They Suggest for Education* (New York: Bureau of Publications, Teachers College, Columbia University, 1949).

liked the books recommended to them. Listed on cards that pupils were asked to check as they returned each book to the library were these items:

I chose this book because it was:
Recommended by a teacher _____
Recommended by a friend _____
Recommended by the librarian _____
Saw it in an exhibit _____
Saw the book on the shelf _____
Read a book note about it _____
Other _____
I liked the book _____
I did not like it _____

Findings revealed that teacher recommendations of books were not very effective. Only 8 per cent of the titles were chosen on the recommendation of teachers and 91 per cent of those recommended by the teachers were disliked by the respondents. When the librarian was asked how he planned to use these data, he replied that he would not reveal his findings since he would lose the cooperation of the teachers if he did so. They would resent the implied criticism.

Until a staff can assess a program without defensiveness, can determine the kind and degree of change desired, explore and plan the means, carry out plans, determine effects, revise and replan, little improvement in school programs can be expected. But fortunately an increasing number of school staffs the country over are gathering all kinds of data, are analyzing these data to discover how effective their present programs are and, on the basis of the evidence, are replanning reading programs.

FORMULATING OBJECTIVES AND DEVISING MEANS

Such stock-taking inevitably leads a school staff to a re-examination of objectives. This is a step that is difficult for teachers to take. They want action and often they are disturbed by the time and effort expended in a study of objectives. Yet ultimately every school staff must face the task of getting agreements on goals which, in turn, are to be spelled out concretely in the content of instruction.

Agreements are easy to reach about the broad goals of reading. Teaching children how to read, how to acquire the primary skills involved in the identification and understanding of words and their meanings is widely accepted as one of the major goals of the public school. The extension and promotion of reading as a tool for learning, and for lifelong self-growth and fulfillment, are likewise regarded as major responsibilities of the school.

Difficulties come, however, when the school staff attempts to reach agreements about how these objectives are to be achieved. Yet there is little point in considering the one to the exclusion of the other since the ends pre-exist in the means.

Assuming that a school staff agrees that in developing a curriculum major emphasis should be directed to the extension of reading as a tool for lifelong learning, what makes achievement difficult? Several reasons can be suggested:

1. Broad, over-arching, long-term goals give little direction to programs of action. Specific objectives directed toward the learning desired for pupils need to be formulated, and on these it is sometimes difficult to get agreement as educational philosophy as well as methods of teaching are directly involved.

2. When agreements are reached on goals, school staffs often do not plan means appropriate to or in agreement with stated goals.

3. There is a tendency on the part of teachers and librarians alike to continue using procedures and devices long after the collected evidence indicates that they do not achieve stated goals.

The writer has often observed with what abandon cadet librarians list teaching objectives in their lesson plans, only to ignore them as they plan teaching procedures. One young woman, when asked how she planned to achieve such an objective as "improving human relationships" in demonstrating and teaching the arrangement of letters in the alphabet to her second graders, shrugged and said, "I list objectives because my supervising librarian likes them."

Once a school staff has agreed on a number of objectives they proceed to initiate plans for achieving them. It is here that the viewpoints of a staff leave their identifying mark on the program. For example, many teachers and librarians are convinced that children will develop an interest in reading when provision is made for "free reading." They make books accessible to children. They expose pupils to books. They schedule pupils to the library for free reading periods and discourage any kind of guidance. Games, activities, and devices for introducing books and promoting interest in reading are used, but little thought is given to continuity or sequence of learning experiences.

An evaluation of these means often produces results that are far from encouraging. "Free reading" appears to result in considerable activity that is desultory and pointless. One observes a number of pupils in a classroom listlessly turning pages of books and magazines. They have been told by their teacher to get a book and read when they finish lessons. They seem to hold the activity in the same regard as does the teacher. It is a way to consume free time.

School librarians observe some of this behavior among pupils who aimlessly turn pages, furtively read comics, wander around and stand in front of library shelves, not browsing, but "putting in time." The causes of this behavior are many. Often the child does not read because he cannot read, but more often he does not read because his purposes have not been mobilized. He has no problems to solve, no answers to seek in his reading. Teachers and librarians alike in these situations have assumed that he will become a skillful, interested reader if he is given a chance to read. They sometimes continue this procedure year after year, never pausing to ask, Does this really work?

In another situation staff members agree that their pupils must become skillful readers. They plan reading programs that place heavy emphasis on reading for information, on collateral

reading, reference, and "work" reading. Book reports are required and credit is given for the number of books read. In these
schools "recreational reading" in the library is often discouraged
during school hours. Teachers are conscientious in their attempts
to promote interest and skill in reading, yet the program seems
permeated with the idea that reading for information and reading
for pleasure are mutually exclusive. Although one would not disagree with the objective, he might question the appropriateness
of the means.

It is not unusual for teachers of English to affirm that one
of the major purposes of their reading program is to develop a
love of reading, yet at the same time they require students to read
from a prescribed list and write long book reports. The overwhelming evidence that these means tend to create feelings of
dislike and actual hatred of books among high school pupils appears to make little difference to them. Year after year the
program is continued, and when responsibility for its failure is
assessed teachers invariably mention the lack of industry and
interest of pupils.

How do these illustrations add up? What do they demonstrate? They indicate that teaching objectives influence what is
done and the way it is done, and that coincidentally with the
examination of objectives a school staff needs to come to some
agreements on how the goals are to be achieved. Staff members
need to identify the specific learnings they wish for their pupils,
detail appropriate means, and pursue relentlessly the evaluation
of the means in relationship to stated goals.

Efforts to plan a total school program should not result in
such strict uniformity that every teacher pursues the same reading
activities. Reading as a tool in learning serves many purposes,
some of them unique to different subject fields.

John Michaelis states that some of the specific purposes for
reading social studies material are:

To get information and secure ideas
To get answers to questions
To learn about far away places

    To identify, clarify, and solve problems
    To make more intelligent choices
    To check on opinions and suggestions
    To verify information [4]

Russell suggests that reading in literature classes is directed toward such goals as:

    Extending experience
    Re-living and re-experiencing the adventures of others
    Developing insight into one's own personality
    Gaining ethical values
    Understanding the problems of others
    Developing love of country and democratic ideas [5]

Clarence Evaul states the purposes of reading in science as:

    Developing vocabulary and phraseology which are peculiar to science
    Gaining skill in comprehension
    Gaining understanding of symbolic language
    Acquiring knowledge [6]

According to Margaret Lehr, "In reading mathematics you are meant not to acquiesce but to agree or disagree." [7]

Dora Smith, discussing several purposes of reading, emphasizes those that relate to personal and social goals. She believes that reading experiences should be planned:

    To help young people gauge themselves accurately, to understand the motives of human conduct in general and their own in particular.

    To understand the ever widening and deepening problems with which life challenges them.

    To increase their awareness of spiritual and esthetic values.

    To contribute to their social adjustment and their understanding of others.

    [4] John U. Michaelis, *Social Studies for Children in a Democracy* (New York: Prentice-Hall, 1956), p. 321-335.

    [5] David H. Russell, *Children Learn to Read* (Boston: Ginn & Co., 1949), pp. 282-285.

    [6] Clarence B. Evaul, "Reading in Science," *The Road to Better Reading* (Albany, N.Y.: Bureau of Secondary Curriculum Development, State Education Department, 1953), p. 57.

    [7] Margaret Lehr, "Experiment with Television," *American Mathematical Monthly*, LVII (January 1955), 18.

To give them understanding of our national culture and extend their sympathy with people whose culture and background are different from their own.

To aid them in learning the basic causes of dissension among men and nations, and to assist them in an intelligent analysis of their own prejudices.[8]

High in the lists of goals in reading is the one related to the development of appreciation and love of books. It is this goal that has inspired the non-directive approach to reading guidance and the "free reading" programs undertaken in many schools, with such attendant assumptions as, "children learn to like to read by reading"; and "children will read if books are made easily accessible to them, if they are given the opportunity to read." It is possible that this goal is a better servant than master, since liking to read may be a by-product of skillful reading rather than a major goal. In any case the goal is far too intangible and encompassing to provide direction in planning and devising reading experiences for boys and girls.

Moreover, it assumes that the act of reading itself is an absolute "good." Lois Lenski suggests that reading is of little value to those "many children who learn to read glibly with their eyes, and even aloud with their lips but never with their minds." [9] She concludes that the primary purpose of books is to enrich our thought, to enrich both knowledge *and* understanding.

From a variety of objectives a school staff will select those goals they consider most crucial in the learning of their own pupils. Individual teachers, including the school librarian, will consider also the specific functions of reading in their special areas of the curriculum. These purposes become the direction-finders, the beacons in the school's reading program. Then appropriate means can be devised and evaluated in terms of the stated goals, and reading programs will tend to be more realistic, more useful, and more rewarding.

[8] Dora V. Smith, "Nature of the Reading Program to Meet Personal and Social Needs" in *Promoting Personal and Social Development Through Reading* ed. by William S. Gray. (Chicago: University of Chicago Press, 1947), pp. 11-13.

[9] Lois Lenski, "Can a Child Think?" *Education,* LXXV (November 1954), 143.

Providing Reading and Library Facilities

To make reading materials easily accessible and to provide an effective reading environment in a school require facilities and organization, which are realized in great measure through the provision of the school library and the services of a skilled librarian.

The Central Library

No longer is it necessary to extol the advantages of having books and other learning materials organized and maintained in a central library. The school library is now accepted as an indispensable teaching-learning unit in the school. The fact that 65 per cent of all elementary schools and 90 per cent of all secondary schools in the country have some kind of school library is witness to its usefulness.

In modern schools the library is one of the most attractive rooms in the building, arranged and maintained to tempt the most reluctant reader. The room is usually centrally located with seating capacity for one tenth of the school population. In small schools (under 400) floor space should be sufficient to seat the largest class group plus 20 pupils and never less than 15 per cent of the total school enrollment. Included in the library suite should be four to eight small, sound-proofed, glass-enclosed conference rooms so that groups of pupils from class and grade rooms can work and plan together with materials close at hand; a classroom where audio-visual equipment is stored and where teachers can bring their classes to view films and filmstrips and to learn how to use library materials; and a large and well equipped workroom for the library staff.

Provision needs to be made for adequate shelving, for built-in catalogs and files to house pictures, pamphlets, records, recordings, films and filmstrips, posters, and other audio-visual materials. In central schools where the library serves pupils from kindergarten through the twelfth grade, one section of the room, preferably a separate alcove, should be equipped with suitable furniture and special shelving to provide appropriate quarters for the primary school children.

Library furniture should include tables and chairs, exhibit and display cases, magazine and newspaper racks, a number of bulletin boards for displaying such materials as posters, book-lists, pictures, models, and books. Informal furniture should be provided for browsing corners.

The book collection needs to be sufficiently large to take care of requests for classroom collections and to provide, as far as it is possible to do so, for unrestricted circulation of materials for out-of-school reading. Secondary school standards accepted by the National Education Association and other regional accrediting agencies suggest a minimum of five books per pupil for small schools and three in larger schools. Two dollars per pupil is the suggested annual expenditure for library materials, at least until the collection reaches a minimum of five books per pupil, when $1.50 is suggested as adequate.

Given an adequate collection, the librarian can organize a circulation system that makes it easy for both teachers and pupils to borrow materials. Actual circulation routines can be put in the hands of a well trained student staff, who, with adequate training and guidance, can help their classmates in the selection and use of library materials, can process new books, and publicize library materials. In most large schools pupils and teachers alike would be restricted in their use of instructional materials without the services of a student library staff; and the librarian who can, without exploiting their services, teach them to work together in the service of others has provided them with one of the most effective learning experiences they will have under the guidance of the school. At the same time he has expanded immeasurably the reading facilities and resources in the school.

Classroom Libraries

The name *classroom library* has a pleasant connotation since it suggests the ideas of boys and girls in their own classrooms working in easy reach of printed and audio-visual materials. Often in self-contained classrooms there is a special library corner equipped with shelves for books and magazines and with tables and chairs for browsing.

This is an admirable situation if materials are circulated from a central library in a school, to be kept only as long as they are needed and then to be replaced. Permanent classroom collections as substitutes for the central library are often inefficient and wasteful. If, in addition, the teacher is not adequately skilled in the use of materials, the classroom collection deteriorates into utter uselessness. Worn books and tattered magazines are strewn about shelves and tables. Faded book jackets adorn the bulletin board, and the library corner is used by pupils as a place to kill time when their school work is finished.

Even when the classroom library is well organized and maintained, it should be used only in conjunction with the central library. In schools that organize the curriculum in units, librarians are sometimes expected to send "forty or fifty books to the classroom" for the duration of the unit. This undoubtedly saves time, but it produces a kind of spoon-feeding of materials to young people. Often they do not find or use materials that have authority and reality for them, nor do they experience the learning that accrues when they themselves explore and select materials from a large library collection.

The library as a materials center is not merely a repository of books that circulate to classrooms. It is a center where children learn to read and to use materials skillfully. For the most efficient use of learning materials, a school will maintain a central library, and collections will circulate to and from classrooms as the needs of the curriculum dictate.

Scheduling Reading Activities

No organizational pattern for using the library and for facilitating reading guidance can be blueprinted for a school. A staff must tailor its own schedule to provide the time and opportunity for its young people to read. However, a number of schedules and patterns may be suggested to provide general direction.

Many elementary and junior high schools assign all pupils to the library for one or two periods a week in the same way that they are assigned to the gymnasium or shops. This assumes that the librarian, like any other teacher, plans carefully for each class, taking into account all the factors that influence learning. The major advantage of scheduling classes into the library is that every pupil in the school has continuous access to books. On the other hand, it results in a work overload for the librarian and lack of access to the library for other groups of children at the moment that they may need to use materials. Nor can the librarian handle sudden requests from teachers. With a full schedule of classes the librarian carries the same teaching load as the teacher. This leaves him with little time or energy for building and maintaining the collection or for working with teachers.

The combination study hall-library schedule that operates in some high schools has the same advantages as the scheduled library periods in that every pupil in the school gets to the library. There are disadvantages in this plan that should be examined. The students who are scheduled to the library during "free periods" regard the library merely as a study hall. Moreover, the librarian finds it impossible to plan group guidance activities, and individual guidance can be provided only when the number of students in the room is sufficiently small to obviate the necessity for the librarian to spend all his time in student accounting.

Librarians who operate the library on a flexible schedule believe that such a schedule facilitates wide and effective use of the library. Teachers schedule their classes to the library for a specific period, and the teacher and librarian together plan the kind of experiences that, in their judgment, meet the special needs of the group. Teachers may have a variety of purposes for these visits. They know what specific learnings they wish for their pupils. Pupils may look for information on a variety of subjects, discover new materials on their current interests and hobbies, explore new interests, or have free choice of books. The extension of pupils' interest in biography or poetry or science is often a valid purpose for library reading. This type of schedule also makes it possible for the teacher and librarian together to teach the skills required for the efficient use of materials and to provide effective reading guidance for individuals. Motivation for reading is usually provided by the activities under way in the classroom.

One distinct disadvantage of the flexible schedule should be mentioned. If the teacher has little understanding of the values of reading and of library use, he may deprive his pupils of library experience altogether.

The disadvantages of both the flexible and rigid schedule can be avoided if the library is large enough to accommodate, in addition to the scheduled group, all other individuals or groups who need to use library resources. This assumes, however, that adequate library personnel is provided to work with them.

In some schools complete freedom of access to the library is maintained. Students in many high schools are permitted freedom of admission during periods when they do not have other scheduled classes. Teachers send pupils from their classes without previous notice. This plan provides for a more functional use of learning materials and appears to be ideal.

In self-contained classrooms, the homeroom teacher often plans for reading periods in the classroom and borrows collections of books from the library to use there.

Whatever the organization, its success will depend on the type of instruction in the school, on classroom procedures, on the teacher's knowledge of instructional materials, and on his skill in motivating their use. The librarian's role is equally important. His ability to put the routine administration of the library in the hands of a student staff, to keep in touch with the curriculum, to work closely with teachers and pupils determines largely the success of the reading program.

The inclusion of library periods in the schedule of a school does not guarantee improvement in the interest and skill of pupils in reading. The important thing is what is done and how it is done. A school staff should share in making decisions regarding the schedules to be maintained. The advantages and disadvantages of different plans need to be weighed carefully and agreements reached so that time is provided and reading facilities made easily available to the school population.

WORKING TOGETHER—TEACHER, LIBRARIAN, AND ADMINISTRATOR

In the past, teachers have tended to regard the library as a repository of books and the librarian as a dispenser of them. Often the school librarian defined his role as one of "giving service to teachers and pupils." An enormous amount of his energy was expended in carrying collections of books to classrooms, sending teachers lists of new materials, ordering and fetching books from the public or county library. He cajoled teachers to use library resources. He worked *for* them rather than *with* them.

With changing concepts of curriculum, the school library has come to have unique and distinct functions. True, it is a materials center, but it is more than that. It is a teaching center used by both teachers and librarians to provide effective learning experiences for children. The supervised study that takes place in the classroom is of paramount importance, but the library offers a special kind of learning environment. The room itself encourages reading with its displays and exhibits, posters and lists, its subject or interest arrangement of books. The browsing corners, the informal furniture add to the lure, as does the presence of pupils engaged in reading.

And the librarian, with his insight and understanding of how children grow and learn, with his wide acquaintance with books, with a consecrated determination to make reading an effective tool for learning, teaches children quite as much as the teacher in the classroom. Thus, the modern library not only contains the best ideas in the world but helps its clientele to enjoy and utilize them.

The teacher who does not take advantage of the resources of the school library is wasteful of both material and human resources, for the maximum effectiveness of the library depends on the quality of cooperative planning done by teachers and librarians. The teacher who organizes classroom instruction around problem areas profits by seeking the help of the librarian in building resource units to facilitate the work of the class as they study a particular problem.

The bulk of a resource unit consists of bibliographies, pamphlets, bulletins, card files, charts, maps, pictures, and lists of community resources. But it is more than that. It is an organized collection of resources in which the purposes of the pupils, the teacher, and the librarian are central, plus a listing of all the possible means relevant to these purposes. For example, if a unit is expected to contribute to skill in problem solving and thinking, or to foster certain habits, skills, and attitudes, these aims should be stated clearly as a part of the resource unit, and in the building of these units the teacher and the librarian both share.

A social studies teacher describes such an undertaking as follows:

It was the beginning of a new semester and the pupils of a sixth-grade social studies class were planning with their teacher. They said "What are we going to do in social studies this term?" They discussed world news and pondered on the meaning of such words as democracy, prejudice, citizenship, and social studies. They talked about things that made them mad and things that made them feel good. They discussed newspaper headlines and listed the names of places that were called current trouble spots. They spent time in the school library, and the librarian suggested magazines and books that might help them decide what things they needed to know about to be intelligent world citizens. They talked to their parents and other adults.

This type of planning led them to choose a number of problems to work on, one of which was the United Nations and how it works to get rid of the causes of war.

The teacher, the librarian, and the pupils then began to organize and collect resource materials: books, pamphlets, charts, maps, pictures, films and filmstrips, and lists of community resources to facilitate the study of the problem they had chosen.

The librarian and teacher together made decisions about the possible learnings to be expected from such a problem, the skills to be mastered by the children as they located, used and brought information to bear on the problem.[10]

In this type of cooperative planning the traditional roles of teacher and librarian appear, at times, to be almost reversed.

Chandos Reid defines their roles as follows:

The librarian deals with the materials themselves which form the central part of the educational experience while the teacher uses those materials in developing educational experiences around them. But the preliminary thinking, the understanding of the specific children, the plan for ways of meeting the needs of the group should include both the librarian and the regular classroom teacher.[11]

How, one asks, can these close working relationships be built so that teachers can exploit to the full the use of the school library? What individual responsibilities should be accepted by them? If the librarian is to take the initiative in joint endeavors that involve the extension of reading, how shall he proceed? A number of suggestions may be made.

Action Suggestions for the School Librarian

Make it easy for teachers to borrow materials from the library. Try not to set stringent regulations regarding lost books and the time limits on books and materials circulated to them. One might better lose books than readers. The librarian who restricts the circulation of books and materials because he "fears that the book might be needed by someone else" may aspire to the title of *custodian* but not *librarian.*

Plan a tentative schedule with teachers to insure that all of their classes have many opportunities to use library materials and resources. Accept a fair division of the labor involved in giving reading guidance and in teaching the work-study skills. Decide who shall do what, when, where. The teacher needs to teach many of the skills in the classroom

[10] Betty Johnson, "Critical Thinking" (Unpublished paper, Wayne State University, Detroit, 1956).

[11] Chandos Reid, "Materials and the Curriculum," *Wilson Library Bulletin*, XXV (May 1951), 678-679.

situation. Other work-study skills should be taught by the librarian. Both the librarian and teacher will provide guidance in reading for individuals and groups.

Share with teachers in the selection of new instructional materials, both book and non-book. Make available to teachers lists, reviews, and other aids and tools in book selection. Encourage and use, whenever possible, their book recommendations and requests.

Encourage and invite teachers to talk over their proposed units of work. Do not limit your participation to suggestions about materials. The education of the school librarian provides him with ample skill for sharing in planning the content and the methods of instruction.

Advise teachers of new materials as they are received, and maintain a continuous program for publicizing all library resources and services. Displays and exhibits in the teachers' workroom or lounge room and attractive notes and lists sent to individuals are effective methods of communication.

Urge teachers to bring their classes to the library and to remain with them. It is important that both the teacher and the librarian know what each is doing in providing learning experiences for the same group of children. This is particularly important when a class is doing exploratory reading for a unit of work. The teacher and librarian who together have shared in pre-planning the unit should help pupils in finding and using resources and materials on the problem under study.

Send classroom collections whenever requested and help in every way possible to have these collections attractively organized in the classrooms. Consult with the teacher regarding the circulation of these materials from the classroom.

If space permits, furnish teachers with a special place in the library where they can examine materials. Professional books and magazines should be available. Often a corner in a workroom can be made an attractive place for teachers to work with easy access to library materials.

Take advantage of the librarian's unique responsibility to acquaint new teachers with library resources. Help them locate books on the shelves, the picture and clipping files, the guides to audio-visuals, the special indexes for locating materials in collections. Apprise them of any special resources or services. Explain the organization and schedules for sending children to the library. Ask each teacher what services he wishes. A personally conducted tour of the library is a promising approach to good working relationships.

Guide teachers who do not have an adequate knowledge of books and materials in their own field. The librarian can help them develop skill in the use of these resources. It must be done unobtrusively, but it needs to be done if teachers are to be able to help their pupils use learning tools efficiently.

In publicizing library resources use bulletin boards and displays in halls and classrooms as well as in the library. As far as it is possible to do so, enlist the aid of students and teachers in this enterprise. Open the library to displays of creative work done by pupils in their classrooms. The effectiveness of this kind of publicity tends to be in direct proportion to the participation of pupils in the planning and arranging of the display materials.

In attempts to find out about the reading interests of pupils, their abilities, needs, and problems, work with the classroom teacher in gathering data, share the findings, and plan reading activities and guidance on the basis of the evidence. Try as far as it is possible to do so to come to some agreements about objectives: what both believe is good reading guidance for children and what individual responsibilities each may assume.

Note that the librarian needs constantly to improve his own skills in human relationships, to check his own motivations and values, to attempt to understand the values, drives, and forces that motivate others, thus becoming more effective in working with teachers in curriculum planning and in the guidance of youth.

Provide progress reports to the principal and to the local board of education. Report the effective use of learning materials made by teachers. Emphasize the service aspects of the library rather than the number of books cataloged or lost. Use circulation figures and other data, analyze library resources and library expenditures in relation to accepted library standards. Objective, graphic reporting is convincing interpretation of the needs and accomplishments of the library.

Participate in community enterprises and activities that may in any way contribute to one's understanding of the community structure and to the learning and growth of its youth.

Action Suggestions for Teachers

Some of the previous suggestions to librarians apply equally to the teacher. There are other responsibilities that teachers need to accept if they are to exploit to the full the use of the library in the reading program. The following recommendations should be kept in mind:

In planning learning experiences for your pupils, think of the library both as a source of materials and a place where the pupils are encouraged to read and where they are taught the skills for reading effectively. Plan the time and oppor- tunity for your pupils to make use of the library's resources and services.

Be sure that you are acquainted with all the resources of the library—that you know what is available and where materials are located. Note particularly the arrangement of reference books and of the books specifically related to your field. Locate the current materials, the clippings, pamphlets, pictures and other audio-visual resources. You may note their arrangement and the organized procedures for circulat- ing them.

Try to inform the librarian in plenty of time about ma- terials that your classes may be calling for. You may wish some of these materials placed on reserve to insure fair distribution. Ascertain before making assignments the availability of materials.

As you develop units of work with your classes, depend on the librarian for help in planning procedures as well as in providing resources. Discuss together schedules and organization for using the library. You may send small groups or you may wish to bring the entire class for directed reading and research. You will find that working with your class in the library gives you opportunity for guidance of individual pupils.

If you are not comfortable in teaching reading and work-study skills, call on the librarian for help. There are many printed instructional aids for teaching the use of books and libraries. Make use of them. It will be far more efficient for you to teach certain specific skills that your class will need in locating and using materials than to expect the librarian to do it. For example, if your pupils are studying the United Nations and need to get information in current periodicals, teach them how to use the *Readers' Guide to Periodical Literature* before you send them to the library. The librarian will follow with incidental instruction as it is needed.

Exploit to the full the library as a resource in providing for individual differences among your pupils, particularly for the gifted child.

Expect a great deal of information from the librarian about new books and other materials. Ask for classroom collections whenever you believe it more effective for pupils to work with materials in the classroom under your direct supervision. Do not depend on classroom collections exclusively, as they tend to deprive pupils of the opportunity of learning to use a variety of reading materials and numbers of sources. Try to arrange time for pupils to go to the library regularly for reading and for a variety of reading activities designed to promote real learning. Provide opportunity following such library periods for book talks and discussions in the class-room. It is only when children talk about books, evaluate, generalize about them that they learn from their reading experiences.

Although one would not wish you to spend a large amount of your leisure in reading children's books, remember that you will not be very successful in sharing enthusiastically in the reading interests of your pupils unless you have ac-quaintance with a large number of their well-loved books. By the same taken, you will not be too successful in recom-mending books to them unless you know the pupils and also know their individual concerns, problems, and interests.

Make use of the fact that the child's reading is of great concern to parents, and that the teacher who takes real interest in guiding the child's reading will find it a bridge between the school and the home. It is a part of a school's program that is very easy to interpret to parents, and the teacher and librarian should together plan ways of encouraging parents to read with their children at home.

Action Suggestions for the Principal

As in other phases of curriculum development, the leadership assumed by the principal in the reading guidance program is of paramount importance. Regardless of how effectively teachers and librarians plan together, projects that are undertaken in a school without the encouragement and active approval and participation of the administrator tend to wither and die. There are numberless avenues for the administrator to travel as he assumes his leadership role in the development of a total school reading program. The following, however, relate specifically to the use of the library:

Encourage the staff to organize themselves to work to-gether, and participate as far as it is possible to do so in planning with them.

Expect the librarian to keep you and the local board of education informed through semester reports of library circulation and other statistical data that give some estimate of the use made of reading materials in the school and the library services provided.

Make use of accepted regional and national standards in making decisions about book and library resources needed to carry on an effective reading program and try by every means at your disposal to secure adequate budget, adequate facilities, and adequate personnel to do the job.

Help teachers and librarians to interpret reading programs and problems to parents. Enlist the aid and support of parents in the program.

Give the staff the security that they need as they undertake to develop an effective reading program as they identify problems, re-examine objectives, re-plan, carry out plans, and evaluate results.

Concluding Statement

The initial step in developing a program to promote lasting interest and skill in reading is the attempt by the members of a school staff to clarify their own values and beliefs and to improve their own competence. As they seek to provide continuity and sequence of guided reading experience for children, grades one through twelve, they tend to revise organization and schedules and ultimately to change many of the curriculum experiences provided their pupils. The job calls for staff members who believe that improvement in the school's program is possible, who understand the unique reading problems in their own school, and who have the skill to work cooperatively in the undertaking. It requires resources, facilities, schedules, and a way of working. It demands of a staff some general agreements on objectives, the detailing of procedures, the continuous evaluation of results.

While it is not possible to describe or blueprint a specific reading guidance program that can be systematically introduced into a school curriculum item by item, on subsequent pages some procedures are suggested that teachers and librarians may find useful. They represent a general coordinated approach to reading guidance, an approach that has been tried in numbers of schools with much success.

Problems for Discussion and Study

1. Assume, for purposes of study, that you are to be the new librarian in a central school, grades one through twelve. What kind of library schedule would you organize, and what steps would you take in operating the schedule? What are the criteria that teachers might use in making decisions about library schedules for their classes?

2. School librarians have been described as "intellectual waiters" and "intellectual assistants." Is this a valid description of the ones you know? How would you define the librarian's role in the school?

3. If you were a teacher in an elementary school, how would you plan to extend the reading interests of your pupils? What organization and schedules would you initiate? What specific help would you expect from the school librarian?

4. As a new teacher of the fifth grade, what steps might you take in assuring your pupils adequate reading guidance? Be specific.

5. What standards and what arguments would you use in convincing a board of education to provide adequate library resources in the school? Make a written survey and summary of resources and services needed.

6. From the variety of reading objectives mentioned in the chapter, choose five that you believe most significant and defend your choice. Would it be wise for a school staff to agree on specific objectives or should these vary from teacher to teacher? Why?

7. If you were the only teacher in the school who appeared to be greatly concerned about the reading program, outline a plan of action for sensitizing other staff members to the importance of an effective program. Don't be evangelistic about it.

8. It has been stated by many authorities that skill in human relations is paramount in curriculum organization and improvement. Explore and evaluate what some authorities say about cooperative participation of school staff members in planning a curriculum for children and youth.

Other Suggested Readings

American Library Association, Committee on Post-War Planning. *School Libraries for Today and Tomorrow.* Chicago: American Library Association, 1945.

Benne, Kenneth D. and Muntyan, Bozidar. *Human Relations in Curriculum Change.* New York: Dryden Press, 1951.

Bohman, Esther L. and Dillon, Josephine. *The Librarian and the Teacher of Music.* Chicago: American Library Association, 1942.

Bureau of Secondary Curriculum Development. *The Road to Better Reading.* Albany, N.Y.: State Education Department, 1955.

Cleary, Florence Damon. *The Library in Action.* Detroit: Wayne University Press, 1941.

Corey, Stephen M. *Action Research to Improve School Practices.* New York: Bureau of Publications, Teachers College, Columbia University, 1953.

Cundiff, Ruby E. *Manual of Techniques in Library Organization.* Chicago: Wilcox and Follett Co., 1952.

Doll, Ronald C. and others. *Organizing for Curriculum Improvement.* New York: Bureau of Publications, Teachers College, Columbia University, 1953.

Douglas, Mary (Peacock). *Teacher-Librarian's Handbook.* Chicago: American Library Association, 1949.

Fargo, Lucile. *The Library in the School.* Chicago: American Library Association, 1947.

Gardner, Jewel and Baisden, Leo. *Administering Library Service in the Elementary School.* Chicago: American Library Association, 1954.

Heller, Frieda M. and LaBrant, Lou L. *The Librarian and the Teacher of English.* Chicago: American Library Association, 1938.

Henne, Frances and others. *A Planning Guide for the High School Library Program.* Chicago: American Library Association, 1951.

Henne, Frances and Pritchard, Margaret. *The Librarian and the Teacher of Home Economics.* Chicago: American Library Association, 1945.

Johnson, Byron L. and Lindstrom, Eloise. *The Librarian and the Teacher in General Education.* Chicago: American Library Association, 1948.

Miel, Alice. *Changing the Curriculum.* New York: Appleton-Century Co., 1946.

Rossoff, Martin. *The Library in High School Teaching.* New York: H. W. Wilson Co., 1955.

Siebens, Caroline R. and Bartlett, Warren L. *The Librarian and the Teacher of Science.* Chicago: American Library Association, 1942.

United States. Office of Education. *School Library Standards,* 1954, by N. E. Beust. (Bul. 1954, no. 15) Washington, D.C.: Superintendent of Documents, 1954.

Walraven, M. R. and Hall-Quest, A. L. *Library Guidance for Teachers.* New York: John Wiley & Sons, 1941.

PART II

PROGRAMS IN READING GUIDANCE

Education does not mean teaching people to know what they do not know, but to behave as they do not behave.

—John Ruskin

CHAPTER 5

READING FOR UNDERSTANDINGS
AND VALUES

*There stand your silent comrades, waiting in their ranks.
Choose your man!*

—CONAN DOYLE

There is considerable evidence to support the idea that teachers cannot shape the characters of their pupils by exhortation and verbal precept or inculcate moral and spiritual values by a system of rewards and punishments. Anyone who concludes, however, that the schools cannot teach an understanding of and commitment to a system of beliefs and values should review the achievement of the teachers of Germany and Russia during the 1920's and 1930's. Relying heavily on instructional materials, on biographies, picture books, primers, and readers, they gave their youth a belief in authoritarian principles and a fanatical commitment to a way of life.

Schools in America have been pre-eminently successful in developing self-reliant, skillful people—people with mechanical ability that amounts to genius. There is less complacency among educators regarding the achievement of the social goals of education, the spiritual and moral beliefs and values required for the preservation and perfection of the democratic way of life. Events of the past several years have caused growing anxiety in this country about the values and attitudes of young people, their adjustment and behavior. Parents and the public in general are disturbed by incidents of aggression, delinquency, and mental illness among children and youth and are asking the school what it is doing about the problem.

School staffs studying the impact of social forces on youth and sensing the pressures of the larger society have become increasingly concerned about what children believe and how they behave. As a result, the country over, teachers are seeking ways of providing experiences in the school that will effect improvement in the values and attitudes of their pupils.

Educators agree that beliefs and values are the motivating forces in the individual's life. They influence his behavior. They are a frame of reference for every decision he makes. They motivate high achievement, or conversely, they discourage it. Yet, there is wide diversity of viewpoints among educators about how these values and beliefs shall be taught.

A few insist that the acquisition of values and beliefs is a by-product of good teaching, that the real business of the school is to impart knowledge, and that good behavior will follow naturally.

Others believe that values are caught, not taught, and that the business of the school is to provide a quality of living where relationships between teachers and pupils are deep and rewarding, where each individual is treated as a person of surpassing worth, an atmosphere in which children sense a feeling of belonging, of security and satisfaction.

Still others maintain that a more direct approach is required. They suggest that an understanding of and belief in moral and spiritual values are given children and youth through direct teaching, followed by many opportunities to generalize, to clarify, to test these values in school and community experiences.

Hopkins indicates the wisdom of mediating these viewpoints when he points out that there is a sharp distinction between the way individuals *obtain* and the way they *build* values. He states that they *obtain* their values through contagion, as they experience over and over specific patterns of action in particular situations. He suggests that the individual *builds* values by "thoughtful, deliberative action in all life's situations which he really faces," and that he begins with "his needs which are the basic drives in his conscious behavior." [1]

The educational problems involved in building values are difficult and complicated, and differences in viewpoint on how to

[1] Levi T. Hopkins, *The Emerging Self in School and Home* (New York: Harper & Brothers, 1954), p. 305.

resolve them have led to a variety of approaches. Currently, many projects are under way in the schools directed toward the improvement of mental health, intergroup relations, citizenship, and character education. As participating teachers engaged in these curriculum studies have evaluated the learning experiences provided children under the guidance of the school, they have inevitably been drawn into the examination of the materials of instruction—books as well as non-book materials—and, in turn, into the exploration of reading for improving the behavior and adjustment of pupils.

In order to evaluate these projects it is necessary to keep in mind the basic assumptions underlying the use of books in teaching attitudes and values, namely: (1) books affect the reader—they affect him in a number of different ways depending on a complex of factors within the book, within the individual, and within the situation in which the book is read; and (2) effects appear to be related to the mechanism of identification, emulation, and symbolic gratification.

On subsequent pages a number of studies and projects are described in which books and reading were used deliberately for building attitudes and values and for personality development. The stories of these projects provide answers to such questions as: How did the participants use books and reading to teach values? Did the projects succeed, and are further attempts to teach values and beliefs feasible? How were the books selected? If books are used to "teach values" does such teaching lessen the allure of books for youth? Do authorities favor these approaches and believe further experimentation is promising? What assumptions underlie these undertakings? What general recommendations do they furnish a school staff which is seeking to improve its reading guidance programs?

READING STUDIES AND PROJECTS

The idea of using books to influence behavior is not of recent origin. Consider the Sunday school literature of the early nineteenth century and its efforts to create perfect moral behavior. An examination of textbooks used in American schools from colonial times down to the present reveals to a startling degree the beliefs and ideals that have prevailed in America. These ideals are emphasized in the texts on the assumption that reading affects the child's behavior.

In the 1930's participants in school projects fostering international good will made extensive use of books and reading in efforts to help young people understand others. In several character education studies, character traits were listed side by side with the titles of books. Researchers apparently hoped to mold character by prescribing a diet of books. Needless to say, the projects were not pre-eminently successful.

During the 1940's studies were initiated and conferences were held as educators sought to meet the problem of radical social change and its attendant impact on the social development of youth. In 1947, for example, educators held a reading conference at the University of Chicago and chose as their theme Promoting Personal and Social Development Through Reading. In the published report guidance techniques are suggested, and numbers of book lists are included for boys and girls, grades one through twelve, under specific captions—Books That Contribute to an Understanding of People, Books That Promote Personal Well Being, and Books That Contribute to Aesthetic and Spiritual Values.[2]

More recently, the use of books in meeting basic emotional needs was endorsed by the yearbook committee of the National Society for the Study of Education.

Indicative of the influence of this approach are the captions of the book lists appearing in current educational magazines and book reviewing periodicals—Me and My Family, Getting Along with Others, Books to Grow On—to mention only a few.

Experimentation continues, inspired by the generally accepted viewpoint that books have a powerful influence on the child, that

[2] William S. Gray, comp., *Promoting Personal and Social Development Through Reading*, Proceedings of the Annual Conference on Reading, 1947 (Chicago: University of Chicago Press, 1947).

they may be guides in the solution of the developmental tasks which face him, a meeting ground for the investment of his emotions and for the building of attitudes and beliefs.

Reading for Democratic Values and Beliefs

Participants in the Detroit Citizenship Education Study [3] carried on a number of projects in which all types of literature were used in efforts to teach an understanding of democracy. Projects involved the reading of biographies about American citizens, the reading of fiction depicting the American way of life and the American heritage, and the use of informational materials in tracing the growth and the meaning of democracy. Books were carefully selected and wide reading encouraged. In social studies and English classes time was spent in reporting and discussion. Teachers used opinionnaires and other test instruments in an effort to determine change in the pupils' ability to differentiate between democratic and undemocratic situations as a result of their reading experiences.

During the first year that these projects were carried on, in spite of tremendous effort on the part of teachers and librarians, very little change that was statistically significant occurred in the attitudes and values of the pupils. Instead, pupils often became tired of the very words "democracy or democratic" used so often by teachers and pupils as they discussed their reading. One exasperated ninth grader voiced her reactions in these words: "This school has gone democracy crazy. I cringe when I hear the word."

After the first year participating teachers replanned the projects and sought to improve their own skills before making a second attempt. They formulated a detailed definition of democracy so that they had a fairly adequate conceptual framework of democracy. They classified their ideas about democracy under four headings: believing in the dignity and worth of the individual;

[3] For a full report of the study see Arnold R. Meier, Florence Damon Cleary, and Alice M. Davis, *A Curriculum for Citizenship* (Detroit: Wayne University Press, 1952).

understanding that man can and should govern himself; accepting democracy's privileges and their attendant responsibilities; and using the method of intelligence in solving problems.[4]

Instead of discussing with children vague concepts such as "being democratic" and "democracy," teachers generalized about characters and situations depicted in books in relation to specific manifestations of democratic living—for example, the limitation of individual liberty in consideration of the preservation of like liberty for others. Such vague concepts as democracy and being democratic were seldom used as pupils were given many opportunities to evaluate, to generalize, and to see relationships between the situations encountered in books and the day-to-day experiences about the school and community.

When this was done consistently over a considerable period of time, test results were statistically significant. Pupils were able to discriminate with intensity of feeling between a democratic and an undemocratic situation and to translate understanding and insight into intelligent ways of dealing with others in face-to-face relationships. Thus democratic values and attitudes were taught through the medium of books.

Reading for Democratic Human Relationships

The Dutch Twins,[5] published in 1911, was the forerunner of hundreds of children's books, fiction and non-fiction, that tell a story of peoples—peoples of differing races, nationalities, religions, and economic status. The understanding of the world about them provided children by these books can hardly be overestimated, and the demand for them increases as world events lend urgency to the task of combating hatred and prejudice.

Projects undertaken in the public schools during the 1930's and 1940's to improve intercultural and intergroup understanding placed heavy emphasis on reading. Teachers and librarians sought by every means at their command to have pupils familiarize them-

[4] For a definition of democracy see Florence Damon Cleary, Alice M. Davis, and Arnold R. Meier, *Understanding Democracy* (Detroit: Wayne University Press, 1948), pp. 1-11.

[5] Lucy Fitch Perkins, *The Dutch Twins* (Boston: Houghton Mifflin, 1911).

selves with the contributions made to American culture by all the
ethnic and racial groups that since colonial days have made their
way to our shores. Contests and campaigns were initiated to
develop understanding of South American neighbors, Spanish-
speaking Americans, migrant workers, immigrant groups, and
other minorities. Most of these activities involved a good deal of
reading.

Evaluation of some of these projects produced considerable
evidence to show that information alone will not counteract prejudice or change attitudes and values. A young person does not, of
necessity, gain understanding or concern for the Eskimo people
because he reads that they live in igloos (which few of them do).
Neither does a lad who has deep prejudice toward Negroes change
his values because he reads Tunis' *All American*,[6] excellent as the
book is in its implications for decent human relationships. It is
remotely possible that his prejudice may be increased.

Directors of current field studies in intergroup relations continue to rely heavily on the use of books and reading in developing
an understanding of others. They suggest, however, that the
librarian and the teacher need to be extremely skillful in introducing books that carry messages in intercultural relationships.
The child must never feel that he is being forced to read them.
Moreover, the impact of family and community prejudices on the
child's reading is not to be underestimated. An elementary school
librarian indicates the extent and seriousness of prejudice among
young children, and the caution with which the librarian should
recommend individual titles.

Jasper, the Drummin Boy [7] and *Dr. George Washington Carver*,[8]
beloved by the Negro boys and girls in my school are studiously avoided
by white pupils. *My Dog Rinty* [9] and *Junior*,[10] are taken off the shelves

[6] John Tunis, *All American* (New York: Harcourt, Brace & Co., 1942).

[7] Margaret Taylor, *Jasper, The Drummin Boy* (New York: Viking Press, 1947).

[8] Shirley Graham and G. D. Lipscomb, *Dr. George Washington Carver, Scientist*
(New York: Messner, 1944).

[9] Ellen Tarry and Marie Hall Ets, *My Dog Rinty* (New York: Viking Press,
1946).

[10] Eleanor Frances Lattimore, *Junior, a Colored Boy of Charleston* (New York:
Harcourt, Brace & Co., 1938).

by white pupils, but the moment they look at the illustrations and suspect that the characters are Negro, the book is quietly replaced on the shelf.

These are only isolated incidents, but they show that children react rather strongly to values in books and that the guidance person needs concrete, definite information about his pupils and real skill in selecting and recommending books.

Helen Trager made an analysis of some 22 book lists published by the most responsible agencies in intergroup education. Her purpose was to ascertain if recommended titles were satisfactory both from a literary and intercultural point of view. Of 253 titles on 22 lists only 61 withstood the test when appropriate criteria were applied. Many of the books were rejected by Mrs. Trager not because they were poor books, but because they were inadequate as bridges to greater understanding and belief in American cultural groups. Mrs. Trager concludes as follows:

> Until now we have put our endorsement on all these books, good, bad and indifferent. We have often ignored the need to apply artistry and skill in the process of affecting attitudes and values. Doctrines of hate can be put forward crudely with sledge hammer blows, but understanding, respect and love take root less easily and require gentle cultivation and our best talents.[11]

Lloyd Allen Cook, Director of the College Study in Intergroup Education, takes a more lenient point of view. He expresses concern that all books may be banned if judged too harshly from the standpoint of the social knowledge, sensitivity, insight, and the literary skill with which these qualities are expressed by the authors. He states that no book is good or bad in and of itself, that the crucial factor in the use of books for intergroup education is related to the teacher's skill in handling the books; to his ability to recognize fallacious ideas; and to his experience and familiarity with the problems and the groups concerned. These, Cook asserts, are the factors that determine success in using books to develop understanding of others.[12] Several recent projects provide evidence

[11] Helen Trager, "Intercultural Books for Children," *Childhood Education,* XXII (November 1945), 140.

[12] Lloyd Allen Cook, *Materials Bulletin of the College Study in Intergroup Relations* (Mimeographed. Washington, D.C.: American Council on Education, 1947), pp. 1-5.

that supports Cook's conclusions; namely, that the kind of learning achieved depends on the insight and skill of the teacher or librarian who guides the reading.

The Intergroup Education in Cooperative Schools project, sponsored by the American Council on Education, explored the effects of reading on children's intercultural attitudes. Participants in the project chose themes important in human relations, such as patterns of family life; community contrasts; economic differences; differences between generations; adjustment to new places and situations; how it feels to grow up; belonging to groups; and experiences of acceptance and rejection. They selected a few books that they believed might provide significant learnings in these eight areas and used them with children to increase sensitivity in human relations. Moving slowly, they developed a short list which was first published in 1947 under the title *Reading Ladders for Human Relations.*

Work has continued on the project. Teachers and librarians have extended selections, annotated books, and organized the lists into ladders according to maturity levels. Equally valuable in the latest edition of *Reading Ladders* [13] are the findings concerning the role of books in human relations teaching and the methods of guidance that have been found effective.

The authors warn that skillful discussion of books is a basic requirement for teaching attitudes and values and suggest a sequence of steps to use in book discussions to make it possible for the immature child to identify with the book characters, to provide for an extension of his own experiences, and to clarify different kinds of human relationships.

No claims are made by participants in the project that reading and books will solve problems of juvenile delinquency or race prejudice or international relations, yet they conclude that the printed page can be used to teach attitudes as well as facts and "to teach in the process of entertaining."

[13] Margaret M. Heaten and Helen B. Lewis, *Reading Ladders for Human Relations* (Revised and enlarged ed. Washington, D.C.: American Council on Education, 1955).

The Detroit Citizenship Study also used books such as *The Hundred Dresses* [14] and *My Mother Is the Most Beautiful Woman in the World* [15] to teach skill in human relations. Participating teachers chose books that were imaginative enough to project the reader into the real feelings of others. Often teachers read the books aloud and then initiated and led discussions so that pupils reflected on *why* the characters behaved as they did. The analysis might consist of an attempt to find out the possible cause of the behavior. Pupils were encouraged to draw on personal experiences. Often role-playing was used so that pupils might take the problem situation presented in books and attempt their own solutions. Thus they figuratively walked in the other fellow's shoes. To the immature child, *The Hundred Dresses* may be only a story of a little girl who told fibs about her wardrobe. A skillful teacher can use it as a powerful instrument in helping children examine human behavior.

The use of books and reading to teach effective human relationships continues, and although it is extremely difficult to evaluate these undertakings, findings from many of the projects provide evidence that pupils increased their understanding of others and that in the participating schools human relationships improved. Their efforts may be summarized in the following generalizations:

1. The effectiveness of the learning depends on the vitality and sincerity of the situations depicted in the books and on the pupils' evaluation of characters and situations that could be discussed without embarrassment because the characters were fictitious.

2. Since skill in human relations depends on the individual's understanding of his own motivations as well as the values, drives, and physical forces that motivate others, it would be wise for teachers to help the immature child to understand himself and to understand and accept others. The wide use of books and other instructional materials appears to be one promising approach.

[14] Eleanor Estes, *The Hundred Dresses* (New York: Harcourt, Brace & Co., 1944).

[15] Becky Reyher, *My Mother Is the Most Beautiful Woman in the World* (Eau Claire, Wis.: E. M. Hale & Co., 1945).

3. Little improvement in human relationships will occur unless these experiences take place in a school that is a friendly place where there is a quality of living that affirms the dignity and worth of human personality, where relationships reveal a readiness to search for ideas and to change attitudes and values as the evidence comes in.

Reading to Achieve Developmental Tasks

One of the promising trends to engage the attention of librarians and teachers is the emphasis on the developmental values in books and their possible contribution in helping youth achieve their developmental tasks. To understand fully the implications of the studies of the developmental values in books, one needs first to review the work done by a number of educators and child psychologists who have studied children and the causes of behavior in the total context of children's developmental tasks rather than the separate physical, mental, and emotional aspects of growth. This approach appears to be a rewarding one as it places emphasis on what the child is trying to accomplish because of his maturing body and the pressures of his environment rather than on his needs and motivations. A list of the important developmental tasks formulated by Corey and Herrick [16] is paraphrased as follows:

DEVELOPMENTAL TASKS OF EARLY CHILDHOOD

1. Creating for himself a more infallible system of security.
2. Finding out how to win his place in a group.
3. Achieving skill and competence in motor control.
4. Achieving independence in caring for himself as an individual.
5. Learning the process of belonging to and becoming a member of a family and the social group.
6. Learning to give as well as receive affection.
7. Learning communication.
8. Achieving emotional release through sensory experiences.
9. Learning the realities of physical work.
10. Learning to discriminate, to make judgments.
11. Accepting rules.

[16] Stephen M. Corey and Virgil E. Herrick, "The Developmental Tasks of Children and Young People," in *Youth, Communication and Libraries*, ed. by Frances Henne and others (Chicago: American Library Association, 1949), pp. 3-13.

Developmental Tasks of Later Childhood

1. Broadening the concept of self.
2. Establishing and maintaining a role in the peer group.
3. Gaining independence from adults.
4. Developing the sex role and sense of sexual modesty.
5. Developing further the physical skills.
6. Broadening and deepening intellectual concepts and value systems.
7. Developing intellectual skills and techniques of communication.

Developmental Tasks of Adolescence

1. Coming to terms with his own body.
2. Learning new relationships to his age mates.
3. Achieving independence from parents.
4. Achieving adult social and economic status.
5. Acquiring self-confidence and a system of values.

The above formulation of the developmental tasks provides the guidance person with an index to the problems that confront a normal child in growing up and suggests the kinds of learning experiences that the school should provide.

Havighurst suggests that there are special times in a child's life when he is ready for certain learnings although he may be completely unaware of the developmental task he is trying to achieve, and the skillful teacher will capitalize on these "teachable moments." He warns that when a developmental task is not achieved at the proper time in a child's normal course of development, it will not be achieved well; and that failure in this task will cause partial or complete failure in the achievement of other further tasks, since developmental tasks must be thought of as a kind of ladder which the individual climbs in his progress from infancy to maturity.[17]

The implications of these studies are clear-cut. If the function of the school is to provide assistance to the child in the achievement of his developmental tasks, then it can be assumed that the selection and use of appropriate learning materials may be one of

[17] Robert J. Havighurst, *Human Development and Education* (New York: Longmans, Green & Co., 1953), pp. 1-5.

several approaches, a conclusion that has lead logically to the consideration and study of the developmental values in books.

A number of projects and studies have been undertaken to find out how effective books and reading are in helping the child with the task of growing up. Some of these projects are designed to study the effects of reading, others to identify the developmental values in books and to ascertain how these values may become valid experiences for children in achieving their developmental tasks. Still others are designed to discover how books may be used to help children solve personal and social problems and to adjust to a variety of situations.

Participants in these projects have accepted as a major assumption the importance of the role of identification—namely, that children identify with book characters and that identification operates on a deeper level than imitation or emulation; that they do not merely imitate the hero, they often become, for a time, the hero. It would follow, therefore, that the child reading a story in which the characters meet and solve problems and achieve tasks similar to those he faces gains assistance in achieving his own. At the same time the book will hold high interest for him, since his own problems and concerns are of major importance.

Russell and Shrodes define this type of identification as "a process of dynamic interaction which may be utilized for personality assessment, adjustment and growth." [18]

A significant study in which books are analyzed in terms of their developmental values is going forward at the Center for Instructional Materials at the University of Chicago. For purposes of study, the developmental values in books were defined as elements in a book which serve as an instrument of communication and supply a wealth of experiences which may aid the reader in his choice of behavior.

In a first progress report, Alice Brooks states that when the study began the major question confronting participants was whether the concept was a valid one. Did books really provide

---

[18] David H. Russell and Caroline Shrodes, "Contributions of Research in Bibliotherapy to the Language Arts Program," *School Review*, LVIII (September 1950), p. 335.

stimulus situations which can lead to new attitudes, and guide or change behavior? A list of one hundred books was selected which seemed to reflect current patterns of social experience and an attempt was made to (1) discover whether or not the books were popular with children, (2) find out from the authors, teachers, and librarians what values they believed the books contained, and (3) ascertain what children said about the effect of the book upon them.

Although the evidence is far from conclusive, Miss Brooks enumerates a few "straws in the wind" indicative of study findings.

1. The impact of the developmental values in a book will not produce dynamic changes in an individual. It may contribute to a complex of forces and factors that build values and influence behavior.

2. Socio-economic and cultural factors influence the effect on the child of the developmental values inherent in the books.

3. The values in the book must be appropriate to the developmental level of the child—to the developmental tasks he is trying to achieve—or he will reject the book.[19]

A study of the voluntary reading of 1,256 adolescents and young adults was made by Weingarten in an attempt to discover how reading had helped them achieve their developmental tasks. The respondents were freshmen and sophomores from seven different colleges. They were asked to state how reading helped them in solving personal problems and to name any specific books that had been influential. From 30 to 40 per cent reported that they identified with book characters; that they gained self-understanding; that they tried to develop personal qualities like those of a book character; and that specific books helped them change attitudes.[20] These data, however, should be examined with the understanding that the respondents were evaluating in retrospect the effects of childhood reading.

Katherine A. Pirie, a first-grade teacher, chose twenty-six books which she used in a series of story hours to discover what

[19] Alice Brooks, "Developmental Values in Books," in *Youth, Communication and Libraries*, ed. by Frances Henne (Chicago: American Library Association, 1948) pp. 49-61.

[20] Samuel Weingarten, "Developmental Values in Voluntary Reading," *School Review*, LVIII (April 1954), 222-230.

books meant to her class. Spontaneous comments of the children were recorded on tape. From a careful analysis of the data Miss Pirie concluded that the children identified with book characters through whom they found solutions to their own problems; that the stories provided the "stuff of imagination through which their world could be clarified; and that the books appeared to assist children in determining what was acceptable behavior." [21]

A study by Nila B. Smith provides information concerning the effects of reading. Five hundred pupils in five schools, grades four through twelve, were asked if they remembered any book, story, or poem which had changed their thinking in any way. About 60 per cent reported changes in attitude as a result of reading, and 10 per cent reported changes in behavior. When asked to name books that had influenced their attitudes and behavior no two children, with but one exception, mentioned the same book.[22]

Reading for Personality Adjustment

One of the major problems of guidance confronting teachers and librarians today is how to help children and youth adjust to the pressures of life, how to help them face realistically and constructively, as far as it is possible for the school to do so, the disrupting and devastating experiences often encountered by them in school and in the home and community. To suggest that reading is the answer is absurd. To indicate that reading may be one approach that the skillful teacher can use appears reasonable, and it is this viewpoint that is motivating the attempts made by many teachers and librarians in guiding and directing reading activities. The current projects appear to be of two kinds: those devoted to using books to help the average normal child with his personal problems and those that encourage reading as therapy for the emotionally insecure.

[21] Clyde Martin, "But How Do Books Help Children?" *Junior Libraries,* I (October 1, 1955), 83-87.

[22] Nila B. Smith, "The Personal and Social Values of Reading," *Elementary English,* XXV (December 1948), 490-500.

Since the early 1900's considerable use has been made of books and reading as therapy and carefully selected libraries are now maintained in most mental hospitals. Psychologists and psychiatrists have found that when the seriously troubled person lives out the emotions of the book character he gets relief from his own anxieties and aggressions—hence the term bibliotherapy, meaning planned reading for mental health.

Psychologists at the Child Center of the Catholic University of America have made considerable use of bibliotherapy in working with problem children. Clara Kircher prepared for the psychologists a graded list of books for children and youth and indexed them under character traits.[23] In the introduction to Miss Kircher's book, Thomas Moore writes as follows:

> It appears that one can introduce ideals and principles into the mind of the child much more easily by bibliotherapy than by verbal instruction and persuasion. The child discovers the ideals and principles for himself. The emotional interest of the story gives them a warmth, a coloring and a beauty that awaken admiration and a desire to imitate. The patient identifies himself with the hero and takes unto himself for a time, at least, the ideals and aspirations of the hero. Conversation with the therapist enables the child to make these ideals permanent acquisitions.[24]

Studies in bibliotherapy yield contradictory results, and reading as a method of treating mentally disturbed people must still be regarded as experimental procedure. Moreover, since studies provide confirming evidence that personality difficulties and reading retardation often go hand in hand, the complexities of using reading as therapy with children are increased. Favorable results appear to depend upon three factors: the skill of the adult in helping the child relate situations in books to his own problems; the vitality and sincerity of the books which the child enjoys as good stories; the rapport that the therapist first establishes with the child.

[23] Clara J. Kircher, *Character Formation Through Books. A Bibliography* (Washington, D.C.: Catholic University of America Press, 1945).
[24] *Ibid.*, p. 10.

Leaving the use of bibliotherapy with the disturbed child to the psychiatrists, educators find that the use of books in helping normal youth meet their problems appears promising. As teachers have acquired techniques for finding out the needs and concerns of youth through the use of checklists and questionnaires, and as they have examined the mechanisms by which behavior can be modified, they have found literature and books rich in situations which parallel those in which young people find themselves.

Several studies have been made in which teachers have sought to discover the fears and insecurities of their pupils and to utilize literature to help solve these personal and social problems.

A project carried on in a small city high school in Michigan is illustrative. The school librarian and a number of high school teachers determined to do something about the values and attitudes of their pupils, many of whom displayed a good deal of atypical behavior and appeared to be in need of counseling and guidance. They set about gathering background information. One of the several checklists they used provided overwhelming evidence of the many very real and serious problems faced by their pupils. Using all the accumulated data as a basis for selection, the librarian compiled lists of appropriate books under such headings as My Family and Me, School Life and Me, Life and Me, and Love and Stuff. Considerable publicity was given the lists in displays about the halls and classrooms and in the school paper. Teachers and the librarian recommended these books with discretion, since they were aware that no adult can suggest such a title as Barber's *The Trembling Years* [25] to a girl who is crippled by polio unless he has the complete confidence and regard of that young person, nor can a teacher recommend to a boy from a broken home a book like *Walk Like a Mortal* [26] unless his relationships with the boy are close and rewarding.

During the first few months of the project very little group discussion was attempted. Guidance was on an individual basis. Gradually pupils began to talk about their reading in English

[25] Elsie Oakes Barber, *The Trembling Years* (New York: Macmillan Co., 1949).
[26] Dan Wickenden, *Walk Like a Mortal* (New York: William Morrow & Co., 1940).

classes and as confidence grew, class discussions were carried on with the young people taking the initiative in interpreting what they read and relating it to life situations.

Participating teachers were convinced that with many individuals improvement in attitudes and behavior occurred. They were equally gratified by the high interest with which a large majority of pupils read—pupils who previously had been extremely bored with books. In evaluating the undertaking the librarian makes this statement:

> Rarely does the high school student have the opportunity or the desire to discuss in his classes the kinds of everyday personal and social problems that confront him. The average youth is far too inhibited to discuss his personal problems in class. But give him a printed prototype through whom he may project his own problems and the way is open to him for a frank discussion with his peers. To the guidance expert and the school psychologist must be left the problems of serious maladjustments and personality conflicts. But the high school teacher or librarian can help the students to develop a clearer outlook on the ordinary vexations that cloud his days. She provides books that give him not only temporary escape but permanent values.[27]

What, one asks, may be concluded from the research relating to the developmental values in books and their effects upon the reader? Certainly there should be no assumption that the developmental values in a book will suddenly cure deviate behavior, change values, or even reinforce valuations and attitudes. Neither should it be assumed that teachers and librarians have not used the values in books for teaching purposes for many years.

The advantages of the developmental approach lie in the way it provides automatically for continuity and sequence of reading experience and for more useful and realistic learning, because books are selected that relate to immediate needs and concerns. When young people are guided and directed to books that depict characters who face the same kinds of problems and situations that confront them, they respond with interest. The reading experience has reality and meaning for them and in many cases, if they are helped in relating these experiences to their own problems, changes

[27] Katherine Rebone, "Books to Meet Students' Personal Needs" (Unpublished paper, Wayne University, Detroit, 1952).

in attitudes and behavior, in ways of thinking may result. Mute proof of how great is the need of young adolescents for help with their developmental tasks is the tremendous popularity of books like Daly's *Seventeenth Summer*,[28] Rawlings' *The Yearling*,[29] or Pinkerton's *Hidden Harbor*.[30]

Learnings, Assumptions, and Recommendations

What, then, has been learned from all of these projects? There appears to be little disposition on the part of the participants to assume that reading the right book at the right time will build values or effect significant changes in the child's behavior. Moreover, evaluation of the effects of reading is difficult since cause and effect relationships are almost impossible to isolate or assess.

There is sufficient evidence, however, to suggest a number of cautions, assumptions, and recommendations that may be useful to the person who is seeking to improve his own skill in guidance.

1. Never should children lose "the song of the nightingale," the magic of good books. They must continue to read "for the story, not the message." Their learning will come through the appeal of situations, the way problems are resolved by book characters, not by moralizing or discussing behavior. There is a trend toward the production of books which are designed to provide for specific learnings but which lack the vitality and sincerity of good literature. These books should be avoided just as "moralizing" about them must be avoided, or plans for their effective use will fail, as fail they should.

2. Books and reading are a rich meeting ground, a promising focus for teaching understandings and values, for aiding youth with their developmental tasks, their problems and concerns, for helping them to understand their own behavior and the behavior of others. For teachers and librarians success depends on the knowl-

[28] Maureen Daly, *Seventeenth Summer* (New York: Dodd, Mead & Co., 1942).
[29] Marjorie (Kinnan) Rawlings, *The Yearling* (New York: Charles Scribner's Sons, 1938).
[30] Katherine Sutherland Pinkerton, *Hidden Harbor* (New York: Harcourt, Brace & Co., 1951).

edge of appropriate books, on their understanding of the developmental tasks of childhood, and on the quality of the guidance that aids the child to relate the situations encountered in books to his own needs.

3. One of the most important by-products of this approach to reading guidance is increased interest in and love of books. When a child meets in the pages of a book a person grappling with the same problems and tasks as his own, the chances are that the book will hold tremendous interest for him.

4. Members of school staffs will experience little success in teaching values and beliefs until there is built in the school an atmosphere, a quality of living, where relationships between pupils and teachers are close and rewarding, and where pupils can identify and test ideals and values in concrete situations in the classroom and school. Until some of these values that the youth reads about are reinforced for him in school and community experiences, he is apt to respond to his reading with cynicism. In fact, in adolescent groups the culture of cliques and gangs in their conflicts with society may largely negate the efforts of a school staff to teach an understanding of and commitment to acceptable moral and spiritual values.

5. These findings give the teacher and the librarian insight into the complexity of the task and some confidence that the approach is a promising one. They suggest some modification in thinking. Instead of starting with the books adults think children should read, teachers and librarians should start with the needs of children, and on the basis of these needs search for appropriate books and develop adequate guidance which at the secondary level often needs to be directed toward the modification of behavior— toward the re-education of the child.

Problems for Discussion and Study

1. Review a number of recent research studies in this field. Use Traxler and Townsend's *Eight More Years of Research in Reading, 1955* listed in Other Suggested Readings as a source. What do you think of their summary of findings relating to the possible effects of reading?

2. Use the assumptions and theories on which these studies are based as a guide in deciding what you might do in teaching attitudes and values through the use of books and reading.

3. How would you attempt to discover whether books affect the behavior of young people? Try to formulate a simple questionnaire that you might use to get reactions of junior high school pupils about the possible effects of reading.

4. Use some of the assumptions, implications, and conclusions reached by participants in the projects described in this chapter to formulate specific action proposals for reading guidance.

5. Explore a number of points of view about how schools can teach moral and spiritual values. Do you agree or disagree?

6. Take some of the suggested lists of the developmental tasks of children and youth, and suggest matching values in books. You might list a number of children's books that demonstrate these values.

7. Write a confidential paper on your own early values and beliefs. What did you believe in at the age of five? What beliefs did you hold highly? Have they changed? Were your school experiences influential in helping you to clarify, sharpen or change values? Can you think of a book or books that have influenced your values or behavior?

8. Using the *Readers' Guide to Periodical Literature, Library Literature,* and the *Education Index,* locate a number of recent studies on bibliotherapy. Review and evaluate the findings.

9. A considerable amount of research has been undertaken recently in efforts to study the effects of attitudes, values, personal conviction, and emotions on critical thinking. If one may assume that the teacher and librarian have the responsibility to help young people "handle emotional thinking," it would appear that a promising approach might be through the guidance of their reading. Do you see any possibilities in such an approach? Can you give illustrations?

OTHER SUGGESTED READINGS

American Council on Education. *Intergroup Education in Public Schools.* Washington, D.C.: American Council on Education, 1952.

Cook, Lloyd Allen and Cook, Elaine. *Intergroup Education.* New York: McGraw-Hill Book Co., 1954.

Educational Policies Commission. *Moral and Spiritual Values in the Public Schools.* Washington, D.C.: Educational Policies Commission, 1951.

Gray, W. S., ed. and comp. *Promoting Personal and Social Development Through Reading.* Supplementary Educational Monographs, No. 64. Chicago: University of Chicago Press, 1947.

Havighurst, R. J. *Developmental Tasks and Education.* New York: Longmans, Green & Co., 1952.

Heaton, Margaret M. and Lewis, Helen B. *Reading Ladders for Human Relations.* rev. and enl. ed. Washington, D.C.: American Council on Education, 1955.

Henne, Frances and others, eds. *Youth, Communication and Libraries.* Chicago: American Library Association, 1949.

Hopkins, Levi T. *The Emerging Self in School and Home.* New York: Harper & Brothers, 1954.

Kircher, Clara J. *Character Formation Through Books.* Washington, D.C.: Catholic University of America Press, 1952.

Lindahl, Hannah M. and Koch, Katherine. "Bibliotherapy in the Middle Grades." *Elementary English,* XXIX (November 1952), 290-296.

Martin, William E. and Stendler, Celia Burns. *Reading in Child Development.* New York: Harcourt Brace & Co., 1954.

Meier, Arnold R. and others. *A Curriculum for Citizenship.* Detroit: Wayne University Press, 1952.

Montagu, M. F. *Readings in Helping Children Develop Moral Values.* Chicago: Science Research Associates, 1954.

National Society for the Study of Education. *Mental Health in Modern Education.* Fifty-fourth Yearbook, Part 2. Chicago: University of Chicago Press, 1955.

Russell, David H. "Reading and Healthy Personality." *Elementary English,* XXIX (April 1952), 195-200.

Smith, Dora V. *Communication, the Miracle of Shared Living.* New York: Macmillan Co., 1955.

Smith, Nila B. "Personal and Social Values of Reading." *Elementary English,* XXV (December 1948), 490-500.

Trager, Helen, and Yarrow, M. R. *They Learn What They Live.* New York: Harper & Brothers, 1952.

Traxler, Arthur E. and Townsend, Agatha. *Eight More Years of Research in Reading.* New York: Educational Records Bureau, 1955.

CHAPTER 6

PROCEDURES FOR TEACHING UNDERSTANDINGS AND VALUES THROUGH READING

But Tom got into a book, crawled and groveled between the covers, tunneled like a mole among its thoughts, and came up with the book all over his face and hands.

—JOHN STEINBECK

In this age of Gallup polls and Hooper ratings, of efficiency engineering and laboratory experimentation, educators, like other professional and business people, have come to rely heavily on the findings of research as they seek to improve the learning experiences provided youth in the schools. The reading studies and projects described in the previous chapter provide a valuable frame of reference, a "useful walking stick to help on the way" for those school staffs who determine to use books and reading as instruments for teaching attitudes and values, for giving youth "understanding of the past, insight into the present and direction for the future."[1]

Yet how to implement in practice the findings of these studies is a problem which will be solved only by the creative and inventive librarian and teacher who in their planning consider such practical questions as: Which of the recommendations and outcomes of these studies appear most promising in my own situation? Considering the unique motivations, needs, and abilities of my pupils, what types of reading experiences are appropriate? What goals shall I choose, what means shall I contrive? How can I plan with my pupils so that their purposes are marshaled, their goals achieved? These are not easy decisions to reach.

[1] Dora V. Smith, *Communication, the Miracle of Shared Living* (New York: Macmillan Co., 1955), p. 25.

A librarian in a junior high school indicates the difficulties of translating theory into practice in these words:

> Yes, I believe that books and reading can be important tools for teaching attitudes and values. I agree that exposure to books alone will not make the child a skillful reader. But, specifically now, what more can I do?
>
> For ten years I have encouraged pupils to read with the firm conviction that reading was important and good for people. I have used all the time-worn devices and techniques for promoting interest in books—puzzles, games, exhibits, displays, dramatizations, choral speaking, book reports, book discussions and story telling. I have encouraged browsing and free reading in the library in the hope that these pleasant experiences would put "the right book in the hands of the right child at the right time." I have urged teachers to send pupils to the library for free and recreational reading. I have recommended books by the hundreds. I have been so busy making books accessible to my pupils that I seldom have reflected about methods, or sought to evaluate the results of my efforts.
>
> During the past few months our school staff has been engaged in a study of our pupils, their backgrounds, needs and problems. We have conducted a series of achievement tests and have studied the findings. We have attempted to evaluate the effectiveness of all the learning experiences provided children under the guidance of the school. I am disturbed by our pupils' lack of achievement in work-study skills and by their reactions to our reading program. They are bored by many of the books they are required to read. Over 50 per cent of them report that they do not go to the library regularly and that they don't like to read. These data combined with the findings of other studies disturb me.
>
> I find that I am no longer comfortable in continuing many of the devices and techniques that I have formerly used. I now ask myself, reading for what, activities for what? To fill time? To keep children quiet? To *make* them like to read? My viewpoint has changed about the values in books and the purposes of the school's reading program, yet I don't know how to help our pupils become more skillful, more interested readers.[2]

What are the function and role of the teacher and the librarian in reading guidance? Shall guidance be non-directive and hit-or-miss, or planned and directive? According to the dictionary definition of the term, *guidance* provides some form of assistance

---

[2] From transcribed interview materials and records of the Detroit Citizenship Study, 1945-1950.

which promotes learning, which effects a change of attitude accepted by the individual to the end that he may be better equipped to deal with himself and to live effectively with others. It may be assumed that the term *reading guidance* implies that the guidance person assists in any way he can the constructive process of interaction between the reader and the book that he reads.

Implicit in this definition is a demand for teaching activity on the part of teachers and librarians in helping immature children in the interaction process. It is doubtful whether it is accomplished in "free reading periods" in which children pursue the reading of books which they might read at home anyway. It is doubtful whether games and devices used in isolation will do more than entertain or fill up time.

It is equally problematical whether the provision of "good" environment, the non-directive approach to guidance, is sufficient for a majority of pupils. Although no one would deny the extent or the value of the motivation provided the young person as he steps into a well-equipped and attractive library, there is an impressive amount of research to support the conclusion that more direct guidance appears to be required. How is it to be accomplished?

On subsequent pages a number of suggestions and approaches to reading guidance that have been used with some success in classrooms and libraries are described. The order in which they are presented suggests general sequential steps that a teacher or librarian may wish to follow in providing real learning for children through the medium of books.

Establishing Rewarding Relationships with Pupils

A young person who has little regard or affection for a teacher or librarian is apt to accept with reservation his recommendations of books. Any attempts to provide individualized guidance through the medium of books tend to be ineffective unless relationships between the adult and child are meaningful and pleasant. Wholesome and effective relationships are established when the librarian or the teacher is disposed to accept children as they are, with all their exceptional abilities, shortcomings, and limitations; such relationships flourish when teachers and librarians create in classrooms and libraries an atmosphere of warmth and friendliness, an atmosphere that helps the individual to identify and work toward the solution of his own problems, to accept himself, and ultimately to understand and accept others. Validated by research, these are generalizations that can hardly be ignored.

The first steps are taken in this difficult and slow process when the guidance person gathers background information on his pupils so that he understands their motivations, values, interests, and concerns. Understanding the behavior of his pupils, he tends to treat them differently. He will deal with the causes of behavior, as well as the symptoms. He will not regard the "problem children" or the non-readers simply as trouble makers. They will be studied and worked with as individuals.

Consider, for example, the case of Paul in the school library:

Aggressive and "hard-boiled," he hates books and scoffs at heroes. He refuses to read anything that is suggested, roams around the room, disturbs others, and regards the librarian with disgust. Background information on Paul reveals that during the past three years he has lived in eight different boarding homes, has experienced in his short life little but failure in school and rejection at home. On a problem check list Paul checked such problems as: trouble with arithmetic, family quarrels, trouble with reading, getting into fights all the time, worried about tests, not smart enough, wondering about heaven and hell, sometimes wishing I'd never been born.

When the librarian had the opportunity to examine all this information, she tended to regard him as a boy with problems rather than a problem boy. The data gave her clues for understanding and dealing with his aggressive behavior, the preliminary step along the long road toward helping him solve some of his problems.

Since the school librarian has contacts with such large numbers of children, it is difficult to collect information about each pupil or to know individuals intimately. If the librarian has scheduled classes in the library, he is able to collect a good deal of information about each class by using sociometric techniques and other pencil and paper devices for gathering background information. He will also rely on records kept by the homeroom teachers and counselors.

In addition, he will use every means at his command to build an environment in the library that makes children feel approval and acceptance, that fosters pleasant and gratifying human relationships. One asset of the school librarian in this endeavor lies in the nature of the library itself. Children usually enter as individuals—not as a class. The atmosphere is non-academic, non-competitive. No marks are given there for achievement. No failure threatens. The room is attractive and informal, and if in addition the personality of the librarian is warm and engaging, pupils will like to go there.

The library is endowed with precious advantages. Yet often the right conditions are difficult to achieve in classrooms and school libraries alike. Teachers are almost overwhelmed by the problem of establishing a high quality of living and working together in a school. The very culture of the American school militates against it. Predominantly authoritarian in tradition, the school has tended to emphasize competition rather than cooperation. In turn, competition has a tendency to produce hostility rather than friendliness. The fragmentation of the school day, large classes resulting in mass methods of teaching, the system of rewards and punishments, the rules and regulations, the standards and marks have built a kind of regimented culture which makes deep and close relationships between teachers and pupils difficult. The pupil must have implicit faith in the adult with whom he discusses his problems or concerns, and unless warmth and confidence are present, neither teachers nor librarians have a good environment for guidance of the child's reading or his learning in the school.

Success, therefore, in building rewarding relationships with children depends to a considerable degree on (1) a continuous study of individual pupils, (2) the use of a variety of techniques to understand the structure and behavior of groups, and (3) the application of these understandings and skills in day to day contacts with youth.

Formulating and Using Specific Teaching Objectives

In a previous chapter a good deal was said about the purposes of reading and the goals of a reading program. The sobering problem confronting the teacher or librarian who, day by day, guides the reading of children is *how* to make objectives *operative*. In his pre-service education, he hears a good deal about the importance of goal-setting and the need to involve his pupils in the undertaking. He agrees that all teaching is purposeful in that it is directed toward bringing changes in the thinking, feeling, and acting of the learner, yet when he begins to teach he has the tendency to forget the goals. Then it is that he begins to think in terms of content to be covered and devices to be used rather than specific goals to be reached.

This is the weakness of many of the guidance activities that are carried on in classrooms and school libraries. Librarians have, for example, accepted "learning to like to read" as a major objective of the library program. The goal is a worthy one, but so broad in scope as to offer little specific direction or approach to the guidance of reading. The librarian is able to pursue practically any activity without any guilt feelings about its effectiveness in achieving goals. The result is that much of the guidance pursued by school librarians is haphazard, desultory, evanescent, useless.

In pursuing so pleasant an activity as reading aloud to a class, the librarian or teacher needs to ask himself these questions: Specifically, now, in consideration of the needs and developmental tasks of these children, what specific learnings do I want to provide them? Shall I attempt by means of books and reading to give them a clearer understanding of their immediate environment and of their own motives and behavior? Shall I try to bolster their sense of their worth as individuals or give them a belief in social equality? Shall I try to help them to see, to hear, to be sensitive to the beauty of the world about them? If, for example, I read my first graders the story of *The Four Riders*,[3] will the story, first of all, transport them into a world of imagination and delight as they

---

[3] Charlotte Krum, *The Four Riders* (Chicago: Wilcox and Follett Co., 1953).

hear the story of the old horse, the goose, the gobbler, and the duck? Is that sufficient, or, in addition, can I help them reflect on the values in "sharing the ride"?

Exponents of the free-reading, reading-for-pleasure point of view might contend that "the story is all." But if guidance is one with teaching, it follows that in planning reading activities the teacher or librarian should treat each situation as an opportunity to promote specific, desirable learnings for children. This means that he needs a clear idea of the objectives he seeks.

If the teacher reading aloud to a class has no purpose other than to keep pupils involved in a worthy activity or to give pleasure, or to consume time, he is not likely to provide the same kind of learning situation that he would promote if he planned the experience as a means for meeting some specific needs of his pupils as they identify with the situations and problems encountered in books. Two cases may clarify the point:

Miss Bassett sends to the library for a book to read to her fifth-grade girls, and the librarian sends her *The Hundred Dresses*. She believes that reading aloud to children is one of the best ways to teach them to like to read. She reads the story and when it is finished she asks them if they liked it. The collective answer is, *yes*. If the pupils were completely truthful in their reply, and if Miss Bassett is correct in her basic assumption, then she has achieved her objective, although one might ponder over the quality or value of the learning experience.

Miss Allen is concerned that her fifth-grade group of upper-middle-class pupils get some understanding of the problems of the children who live "on the other side of the tracks." She knows that exhortation about respect for human personality is not very effective. She believes that books can be instruments for teaching values. She chooses *The Hundred Dresses* deliberately because of the author's powerful delineation of the problem of the underprivileged child and his need to gain status with his peers. She reads the story without comment, then skillfully directs discussion so that the pupils reflect about why Wanda, Peggie, and Maddie behaved as they did and what it feels like to be laughed at.

Both groups enjoyed the stories, but enjoyment and interest appeared to be enhanced for the pupils in the second group in so far as they participated in discussion, reached generalizations, and had a chance to examine their own motivations in the light of an imaginary yet realistic situation. The teachers achieved stated objectives, but it is possible that in the first situation pupils did little thinking about the story and learned less from the experience than did the pupils in Miss Allen's room.

In emphasizing how essential it is in planning for the teacher to formulate teaching goals, one must not minimize the need of sharing with pupils in goal setting. Pupil purposes must be marshaled if reading experiences are to be meaningful to them. On the other hand, these should not be the sole determiners of action since there are many learnings that children need of which they may be quite unaware, many potential interests to be developed, and many new fields to be explored. The skillful teacher will exploit to the full young people's present interests, concerns, and problems as a way of marshaling their purposes, but he will, in addition, have other purposes of which the pupils are quite unaware.

The fourth-grade teacher, for example, introduces and reads books like *The Little House in the Big Woods*,[4] *The Courage of Sarah Noble*,[5] and *The Moffats*[6] because he knows that his fourth graders will love them as stories of real boys and girls of their own age. In addition, he recognizes how acute is the need of these ten-year-old pupils to get along with their own family groups, and he knows that these books give them a swift passage into wholesome family living. Thus he uses his pupils' purposes or interests to extend their experience and give them insight into what family life can mean.

PLANNING READING GUIDANCE PROCEDURES

Planning is indispensable in promoting effective reading guidance, although the experienced teacher or librarian does it on an informal basis. He thinks through what needs to be done. He

[4] Laura Ingalls Wilder, *The Little House in the Big Woods* (New York: Harper & Brothers, 1932).

[5] Alice Dalgliesh, *The Courage of Sarah Noble* (New York: Charles Scribner's Sons, 1954).

[6] Eleanor Estes, *The Moffats* (New York: Harcourt, Brace & Co., 1941).

chooses appropriate books; decides how to mobilize the purposes of his pupils, how to present books so that the experience will have meaning and reality for his pupils; helps them to evaluate, to reach generalizations and see relationships to life situations.

This constitutes good planning whether the guidance person is working with an individual or with a class group. Although there are many likenesses between individual and group guidance, there are also differences, and for that reason each is discussed separately.

Individual Guidance in Reading

No aspect in teaching can be more rewarding to the adult than encouraging and sharing in a child's reading interests; and, if time can be found for individual guidance, procedures are relatively uncomplicated and the results gratifying.

The adult who knows and loves books and who lives with a child as he grows from infancy to maturity is aware of the opportunities and compensations of shared reading experience. Reading guidance begins when the adult helps the baby identify the dog, the cat, the bird, or the glass of orange juice pictured in gay colors on the pages of his first book. It is a rewarding activity for the adult, and the baby communicates his delight with every nerve and muscle.

Soon reading centers on the Mother Goose rhymes, and the adult watches the ever-new miracle of memorization as the two-year-old furnishes the last word of every oft-repeated line. Listening to stories at bedtime has, meanwhile, become routine procedure, and current favorites are read aloud with no variations or deletions countenanced. The adult's throat takes real punishment now. There are stories of geese that frighten disobedient scotties, and little engines who think they can. There are tales of princesses and policemen, of trains and tractors.

Soon the child is five, and beginning to read for himself, but shared experience continues as the adult helps him choose books from public library shelves, suggesting, calling significant books to his attention but not dictating his choices. He lives with heroes. He is a knight at King Arthur's court, a Hercules, an Atlas, a Daniel Boone or Davy Crockett. During this period any book of adventure stands high among his favorites as he "sails beyond the sunset and the baths of all the western stars."

Now he is a teen-ager and as the line between reality and imagination becomes more sharply defined, the far-away and long-ago heroes give way to Roy Rogers and Mickey Mantle. And as life begins to have a future in which plans for making a living loom large, stories that deal with the work men do capture his attention. The modern Francis Drakes, and the men who build the bridges, make the laws, win the games, drive the machines, ride beside him now. Speed and action are his watchwords. He reads more books of information, more newspapers and magazines as he struggles to understand the world about him, a world that at times seems close and confining, and again, exciting, vast, portentous.

All too quickly eighteen years pass. The youth is in college and talk about books centers on the merits of a Faulkner, a Farrell or a Joyce, and the psychological implications of *War and Peace.*

Just what has been the role of the guidance person during these years? No single blueprint was followed, but these things the adult did: He made a wide variety of lively and appropriate books easily accessible. He listened to endless accounts of "swell stories." He tried to ask the questions that helped the child to reflect about what was read, and he answered, without equivocation, the questions put to him.

Very early the adult learned never to show surprise at or disapproval of the child's reading tastes or interests. There were a number of times when he accepted the fact that the full month's allowance had been spent for comic books—violent interest, but short lived. And he listened calmly to an announcement made to the startled family at dinner: the child, not quite twelve, having read *Of Mice and Men* (found on mother's bedside table), wanted to know, how about it?

Every step of the way the guidance person helped the child examine human behavior and shared with him through his books as completely as a sympathetic, loving adult can, an "imaginative awareness of human experience."

This is reading guidance not easily achieved in a school situation, yet even here a high quality of guidance can be provided by the dedicated and skillful teacher or librarian.

The school librarian may have contacts with a child year after year. As he watches a child in his normal development and learns to know him well, he can promote continuous growth in reading. Knowing the developmental tasks that the child faces, the librarian suggests books with appropriate developmental values. He knows what the child likes in books and is able to provide a variety of reading materials that build bridges from present interests to potential ones. In a continuous and informal sharing of interests they build, year by year, mutual regard and respect that provide rich ground for individual counseling.

The following are a number of useful techniques in individual guidance:

1. Use what you know about how children grow and learn and find out as much as you can about the individual. Experienced teachers and librarians become adept in learning a good deal about the individual in a brief contact. They note his posture and dress. A few adroit questions interspersed with information about one's own interests help the adult to establish rapport as well as to discover the child's interest and concerns.

2. Recommend several books to him and make it easy for him to make the final decision. On the basis of the child's needs and interests and the general stage of his development, suggest a number of appropriate books from which the pupil may choose. Do not embarrass the child if he chooses none.

3. Talk about books that the child has read recently; talk about them casually and informally but help the child reach generalizations. Astute questions are required to ascertain if the individual has extracted anything of value from the book. Although the child reads the book for the

story, not the message, he will learn to enjoy reflecting and thinking about a book if questions are asked that encourage him to do so. Many reading programs indoctrinate him with the idea that thinking is not required in leisure reading.

It is a difficult task to give individual guidance to large numbers of pupils. Yet one of the major advantages of the school library is the opportunity it gives the librarian to work with the individual. Since reading interests and abilities are highly individualistic and since young people read for such a wide variety of purposes, it is the face to face relationship with an understanding adult that gives the pupil the kind of assistance that goes far beyond "encouraging him to read."

Group Guidance in Reading

Despite the advantages claimed for individualized reading guidance, group guidance may be equally efficacious in promoting skill and interest in reading, for often the group itself inspires enthusiasm and interest. The interaction between young people as they discuss books and reading provides common ground for sharing different viewpoints, trying to understand one another, evaluating behavior, and testing values. The group situation makes it possible, also, for the individual, if he wishes, to remain inconspicuous when values and behavior are probed. The advantages of group guidance are pleasant to contemplate since so much of the teaching that is pursued in the public school must, of necessity, be carried on with large numbers of children.

How should the teacher and librarian plan for group guidance so that real learning is effected? Even in such simple procedures as reading aloud, introducing books, book talks and discussions, planning should be done with painstaking regard for how people learn.

A group of cadet librarians who were seeking to improve their skills in guidance, organized an outline, to provide direction in introducing and discussing books with their pupils.[7]

[7] A group project undertaken during the spring semester of 1951 in a Library Science class at Wayne State University. Members of the group were Ruth Edberg, Nancy Dodd, Carol Lewis, Jane Schettler, and Eleanor Widlak.

Choosing Books and Detailing Specific Teaching Objectives:

1. How does this particular learning experience fit into the long-term learning experiences which this particular group needs?

2. What are the particular learnings the class needs at this time?

3. What stories or books exemplify the values that need to be presented to this group?

Motivating the Learning:

1. Can I relate the setting of the story to something the pupils already know?

2. Can I appeal to present or potential interests of these pupils?

3. Can I set a problem which is real to the pupils and which the story can solve?

4. Are there any new or strange concepts that may be encountered in the story which need explanations before the story begins?

Presenting the Story:

1. Do I know and like the story well enough so that I can read it or tell it well without interruption or further explanation?

Generalizing and Evaluating:

1. What questions can I ask that will encourage pupils to tell what the characters did and why; that will help pupils reflect, make judgments, consider what they might have done in similar situations?

2. Can I help pupils to transfer the values identified in the book to other situations which they encounter—without moralizing or imposing my own opinions?

In planning learning experiences for their pupils, these librarians discovered that they needed always to be alert to the idea that pre-planning often provides only a point of departure, and that their plans needed to be flexible enough to admit changes as the situation dictated.

While they were not disposed to sacrifice warmth and informality as they discussed books with children, they found that there is a vast difference between a situation that provides for spontaneity and flexibility within orderly learning procedures, and one so haphazard and unstructured that discussion about books tends to be on the level of vague generalities. However, they were careful never to go beyond the comments and generalizations made by the children. They avoided pointing a moral.

Assuming that the guidance person knows the expressed interests, needs, and reading abilities of a group of pupils, that he knows what they look for in books, how shall he introduce, discuss, and utilize books so that real learning is effected without spoiling the right of the child to read for fun?

A number of incidents are selected to illustrate some of the problems involved in contriving situations that will promote continuous growth and interest in reading.

Introducing Books

A librarian in a junior high school tells how she introduces books to a seventh-grade class:

When my pupils come to the library for a reading period, I try to introduce a number of carefully selected books. In the past my introductions tended to be like this: Here is a book about a boy who . . . . Recently I have tried another approach. Very casually I ask how they feel about it if their parents sometimes tell them that they aren't old enough to do this or that. Discussion is spirited and problems about using lipstick, going to the movies, driving the family car are quickly identified. Then I mention such books as *A Place for Peter* [8] or *The Wonderful Year*,[9] and suggest that they might like to know what Peter or Ellen did about the same problems.

This approach appears to be far more successful than the *you will like this book* approach. I find that interest in books develops in direct proportion to the way I provide them with books that are related to their own real problems.

The next incident demonstrates how important it is for the teacher or librarian to explain new concepts or situations that might confuse young children and discourage interest in a given book. The situation is described in the teacher's own words.

I found a list of books for primary children with the caption Books to Teach Social Sensitivity, and the school bought all of them. One of the

[8] Elizabeth Yates, *A Place for Peter* (New York: Coward-McCann, 1952).
[9] Nancy Barnes, *The Wonderful Year* (New York: Julian Messner, 1946).

first ones I chose to read to my third graders was *Down, Down the Mountain*.[10] They were bored to death with it and thought Hetty and her brother Hank and what happened to them was just plain silly.

When the teacher was asked how she had introduced the book to her pupils, her reply was, "I told them I was going to read them a story." Her disappointment was apparent, but it did not stem from understanding how children learn. She appeared quite unaware of the need for her group of urban, middle-class youngsters to have some previous introduction to mountain children, before they could be expected to enjoy the story or to recognize that Hetty and Hank were happy children because they were in a family that worked together and loved each other.

Let us travel to another school in a lower-middle-class community and listen to the school librarian as she works with a group of first-grade pupils. Seated in a low chair with the children grouped around her, Miss Bates held McCloskey's *Make Way for Ducklings* [11] in her hand. Quite casually she mentioned having seen some ducks in the park as she walked to school that morning. What kind of ducks were they? Why were they in the park?

Conversation continued for at least twenty minutes about ducks, both tame and wild, and how they are protected; about parks in large cities, those in their own city, and in a city called Boston, which the librarian had visited the previous summer.

After a thorough sharing of experiences, the librarian introduced the book and read the story through. The children listened with rapt attention, and only their gay bursts of laughter occasionally interrupted the story. Later, their spontaneous comments showed how completely they identified with the little ducks who, small and defenseless, had stopped the traffic on the busiest street in Boston.

Because the librarian had previously explained such new concepts as swan boats, mallard ducks, and the Boston Common, the children were ready to appreciate fully the magic of McCloskey's book.

[10] Ellis Credle, *Down, Down the Mountain* (New York: Thomas Nelson & Sons, 1934).
[11] Robert McCloskey, *Make Way for Ducklings* (New York: Viking Press, 1941).

These incidents have been told for only one purpose—to suggest that teachers and librarians alike need to plan with careful attention given to how children learn, and that they need to recognize that the best book in the world will not necessarily suffice if other factors that make a good learning situation are not present.

Discussing Books

There is a vast difference between book discussions that involve the retelling of the story and those that make it possible for pupils to probe into how it happened and why. Nothing kills pleasure in reading more quickly than the certain knowledge that the instant the book is finished the teacher will begin to ask a series of questions designed to ascertain what the book is about.

Stella Center warns against this practice and suggests that the child gains "insights and perceptions of human experience through reading as he develops an awareness of a background, an explosive incident, a sequence of events, a struggle or clash, characters in two opposing camps, a climax, a theme, and a dominating idea or feeling." [12] There can be little disagreement with this idea, but the problem confronting the teacher or librarian who guides the reading of immature pupils is how *awareness* is to be developed. Does it come by chance? That is to be gravely doubted, and the millions of non-reading children and youth bear mute evidence to the fact. Deliberate help must be given before the child sees relationships between what he reads and his own life experiences.

This suggests book discussions that place heavy emphasis on questions of *how* and *why* and *what does this mean to me,* rather than on questions of information. Often pupils become so accustomed to *what* questions about books that they appear confused when demands are placed upon them to think about what they read or make individual evaluations of books.

When they are asked to defend a statement of opinion, they often give such halting reasons for liking a book as: I liked it because it is a good book, or I liked it because it was exciting.

[12] Stella Center, "Begin with the Best for the Young Reader," *Library Journal,* LXXIX (September 15, 1954), 1612-1614.

Yet, when children get a little assistance, they reach generalizations and reveal amazing insight into cause and effect relationships and patterns of human behavior as depicted in stories and books.

A number of questions suggest promising approaches to discussion:

Do you think this story could have happened?

Have you ever seen anything like this happen? When?

Has anything like this ever happened to you? What did you do about it?

What do you remember about the people in the story?

Do you think that people really do those things? Why?

How are you like the people in the story?

Since you and I have talked about the story, do you like the people better?

Is there anything in the book that helps you?

Would you like to live with that family?

Why wouldn't you like to live with this family?

Would you like ———— [the book character] for a friend?

Do you know anyone like ————?

If such an experience happened to you, what would you have done?

How did the story make you feel? Why?

Would you like to be like ————? Why?

Have you ever tried to do what ———— did?

Why did you like the book?

How do you suppose ———— felt about the experience?

To illustrate how a skillful teacher uses discussion to examine values and to evaluate behavior, let us go to Miss Smith's classroom as her sixth-grade pupils return from a regularly scheduled hour in the school library.

Miss Smith suggested that they talk about books they had been reading in the library, and the pupils asked if they might review the list of questions they had previously devised to help them talk about their reading.

As the boys and girls recalled the questions, Miss Smith listed them on the blackboard as follows:

Who is the author and what do you know about his books?
Did the story seem real to you?
What did you like best about it?
If such an experience happened to you, what do you think you might have done about it?

Jack, aged eleven, volunteered to talk about Sperry's *Call It Courage*.[13] Briefly he recounted the story of the Polynesian boy, Mafatu, and his terrible fear of the sea. He spoke of Mafatu's attempts to overcome his fear and appeared to question whether such drastic measures were required of Mafatu to prove his courage.

At this point Miss Smith very quietly entered the discussion. Why was Mafatu afraid? Among Mafatu's people was it a disgrace not to be a skillful fisherman? Why did Mafatu have to be a warrior? Are people without fear truly courageous? Who is a really brave person? Was Mafatu's way of overcoming his fear a good one?

General conversation ensued as the pupils became engaged in attempting to define courage. Others told of war experiences of their fathers and brothers. The class was difficult to manage, as pupils all wanted to talk at once. Miss Smith did not moralize nor did she overemphasize personal fears, but before the hour ended she had helped a number of children draw some rather important generalizations about behavior. Later she evaluated the discussion in these words:

"Convinced as I am that youngsters identify with book characters, and hence accept their ideals and aspirations, I try to capitalize on situations and problems encountered in books in helping them to evaluate behavior, make judgments and clarify values. Pleasantly enough, their interest in books has increased dramatically since I have taken that approach. The pursuit of ideas and the solving of problems can be a thrilling experience for children."

Let no wrong impression be created from these illustrations about when, how, and in what situations discussion about books is appropriate. Many reading periods should be spent in leisurely and quiet reading. Pupils must have time to read in school as well as out of school. Schemes for circulating books should be so flexible that the child who starts reading a book during a reading period in his classroom or in the library may charge the book and

[13] Armstrong Sperry, *Call It Courage* (New York: Macmillan Co., 1947).

take it home with him. All reading and library periods need not be devoted to discussion or other teaching activity. Moreover, there is some literature that does not lend itself to analysis. Although it is true that children obtain but a small fraction of the meaning of a story in their initial reading of it, it is essential that both librarians and teachers plan so that a variety of reading experience is provided the child.

Role-playing Stories

How do the librarian and teacher help pupils relate the situations and characters they meet in books to life situations so that young people can learn to evaluate behavior? How can teachers help children acquire skill in reflective thinking, in saying, what does this mean to me? Among a variety of discussion procedures, one deserves special comment.

Role-playing problem situations in books and stories works well in helping boys and girls discover what it feels like to "walk in the other fellow's shoes," and to identify with persons different from themselves as they attempt to think through solutions to others' problems. Role-playing stories can be enacted without personal embarrassment, since it removes the actual, real-life problem into the realm of books. The learning, however, is dramatic since the pupils themselves participate in working out solutions to the problems encountered by the book characters.

Let us go to an eighth-grade classroom in a small central school in a rural community.

A rather heated argument had been touched off in Mr. Adams' room concerning the incident in Tunis' *All American*.[14] In the book Ned LeRoy, a Negro boy and the outstanding player on the school team, is not allowed to go South to play an intersectional game "because colored boys are not permitted to play with white boys down there."

A number of the boys and girls in Mr. Adams' room had read the book, and most of them held very definite opinions about the situation. One of the boys believed that canceling the game was only to dodge the problem. Another expressed the idea that the individual has to adjust

[14] John A. Tunis. *All American* (New York: Harcourt, Brace & Co., 1942).

to many situations over which he has no control. Another suggested that Ronnie only embarrassed Ned by feeling sorry for him and that he should not have asked questions.

Mr. Adams asked his group if they wanted to play the roles and work out their own solution to the problem, and the sociodrama began. It was evident that the technique had been used previously as a number of children volunteered for roles and "finished the story in action."

Discussion followed as Mr. Adams asked "the audience" how well the members played the roles and how well the problem was solved with respect for human personality. As evaluation continued, other pupils volunteered to replay or demonstrate alternative solutions. At this point Mr. Adams asked if anyone in the group knew anyone to whom this type of experience had happened. He was alert to the need of protecting any individuals in the class from admitting that it had happened to them, but he made it possible for the pupils to share experiences and reach generalizations.

Never at any time did Mr. Adams foist the moral of the story on the group, or leave anyone with the uneasy feeling that "he means me." He used a skillful technique in helping his pupils reach generalizations and evaluate behavior.

Relating Reading to Other Learning Activities

Because books and reading are both a means and an end in education and since reading is involved to a major degree in all of the learning activities and experiences offered children by the school, the teacher and librarian are sometimes perplexed regarding the relation of reading guidance to other learning activities.

The desirability of relating learning experiences is well established, and the adult who is searching for ways to help youth develop skill and interest in reading will exploit to the full other media of communication and other techniques of group guidance. Shadow plays, pageants, marionettes, puppets, radio and television programs, choral reading, role playing, dramatization, book talks, silent reading are all useful. Other media of communication— audio-visual materials, films, filmstrips, records, stereoscope viewers, pictures, book displays—all tend to make learning less abstract. A flannel board can be used by the story teller to build his story sequence graphically. Pictures of book characters, scenes, and settings of stories make reading experiences more realistic and meaningful. Many opportunities can be provided for pupils to participate, to work with books, to plan and organize displays, bulletin boards, book lists, and posters. They may make illustrations or soap models of book characters, collect pictures and stories of authors and their books, write annotations and develop their own book lists. They may share in selecting books, plan programs and book fairs, and use books to motivate many other learning activities and experiences.

Hopkins asserts that each child builds his values by thoughtful, deliberate action in life situations which he faces, assisted by understanding and helpful adults.[15] Reading activities provide many promising situations for youth not only to obtain values by contagion but to build them. A story or book may make a vivid impression on the child—he may never forget the incidents of the situation; but the learnings are strengthened when the vicarious experience is reinforced by action, in face-to-face relationships. The following incident indicates how other learning activities operating in association with reading provided for the testing of values and beliefs in action:

Miss Black considered some ideas that she believed her third-grade pupils should begin to examine. She was planning their Christmas party. Pupils would exchange simple gifts and she would buy the Christmas candy and together they would decorate a tree. The day before she had come upon a little story that suggested the values in giving to others. It recounted the difficulties of two little children in finding a gift for their grandfather that he would really enjoy. He was ill and rather lonely. They had very little money to spend. So they built and placed outside his window a bird house and feeding station, and grandfather spent many happy hours in bird watching.

She read the story without comment and listened to the conversation that followed. One child suggested that he would like to make a bird feeding station for his grandfather though he doubted whether his grandfather would have time to watch birds. He was too busy. Other comments followed. At length a small boy suggested that it would be fun to make

[15] Levi T. Hopkins, *The Emerging Self in School and Home* (New York: Harper & Brothers, 1954), p. 305.

a bird house and give it to someone. At that point the teacher asked whether anyone knew an older person who might enjoy such a gift and whether they could build a bird feeding station in their classroom. With that question she set a problem, and teacher-pupil planning began.

The next three weeks were busy ones for Miss Black and her third graders, but on the afternoon before Christmas the school bus took them all out to the County Home to give the old people there a real Christmas celebration. The children presented the bird houses and feeding stations which they had constructed and the candy and popcorn balls they had made. They sang Christmas songs and dramatized some Christmas stories. For a time many of the children were shy with the old folks, but gradually the strangeness disappeared. It was a never-to-be-forgotten party for the old folks and for the children.

A skillful teacher had used a simple story to provide a situation in which children not only gained knowledge and skill, but tested some fairly important values in action.

These opportunities are provided in both in-class and out-of-class activities in schools earnestly concerned in helping with the adjustment and behavior of children and youth. Such opportunities become teaching content for examining and learning about human needs and motivations and their expression in everyday behavior. It is in these situations that young people test the values that they discover in their reading and by testing them in many situations are committed to them.

A Summary

The plans and procedures described in this chapter are not offered for the purpose of cajoling and luring children to read as if reading were a game. Nor are they presented as techniques to change behavior through reading. Certainly, the roots of behavior are not reached by devices or by simple exposure to books.

These programs should be considered as ways of working that librarians and teachers have found helpful in making meaningful and useful the vicarious experiences boys and girls find in books. They may suggest ways of providing assistance to pupils in using reading as a rich investment for their interests, needs, and concerns.

Although it seems fair to assume that books and reading provide abundant ground for teaching values and attitudes, skillful teachers and librarians refrain from doing so along too narrow a path lest reading guidance become a method of indoctrination and a didactic exercise. When one considers that a child's reading is influenced not only by a combination of factors, such as intelligence, sex, environment, and emotional adjustment, but by complex relationships among these factors, it follows that no clear-cut, simple plan for promoting and guiding reading can be blueprinted.

Somewhere between the extremes of the directive and the non-directive approach to guidance appears to be firm ground on which to stand. Certainly, if the immature child learns to love to read as he really learns how, it follows that parents, librarians, and teachers need to provide the kind of guidance that encourages him to read with his mind as well as his heart.

PROBLEMS FOR DISCUSSION AND STUDY

1. Margaret Scoggin in *The World of Children's Books* makes this statement:

Wishful adults believe that a "good book" has in it something magical and if anyone can be dragged through it, he will automatically become a better man! . . . The magic is not something in a book; it is something that can take place between a reader and a book.

Explain and clarify this statement. What are its implications for the teacher or the school librarian?

2. A good many educators are convinced that literature should stand the test of the child's approval and that in the selection of literary materials the interests of boys and girls should be the major consideration. In his writings Joseph Wood Krutch has presented a different point of view, indicating that it is the duty of teachers to select the great books of the world and teach students why they are great. He rejects the idea that guidance in reading should be directed toward "bringing literature to children" rather than "bringing children to literature." He writes as follows:

Indeed it is difficult to see just what we are supposed to be getting in return for all the money spent on schools if school children spend their time reading what they would read anyway. It might be argued that the teachers were learning something from the pupils; namely, what the taste of the uneducated children is. But the pupils were certainly not learning anything from the teachers, and it would seem that the children are the ones who ought to be paid salaries, if anyone is to be.

Do you agree or disagree? Why? You may wish to read the article which appeared in the New York *Herald Tribune Book Review*, XXVII, (July 22, 1951), 3.

3. The school library offers special advantages to the gifted child. Discuss at length individual guidance that the librarian can provide to challenge the child's abilities and to encourage and extend the learnings provided in the classroom. You may wish to do some reading on the subject.

4. In many elementary schools pupils are scheduled to the library for reading exactly as they are scheduled to other classes. How would you insure them a developmental reading program in the library? How would you provide for continuity and sequence of reading experiences? What might be some of your objectives? Make some tentative plans for one class for a semester.

5. For many years activities, games, and devices have received considerable emphasis in courses of study. School librarians have talked about reading guidance in terms of activities and devices and have collected all kinds of pleasant procedures, games, puzzles, and techniques for stimulating "interest in books." Could you suggest ways that these might be used more effectively?

6. Often when a few pupils finish assigned work ahead of others, the classroom teacher suggests that they "read." Indicate procedures or methods to insure that this type of activity is profitable rather than time filling.

7. What means would you suggest for attempting to encourage and help parents to read with their children at home?

8. In *College English*, XV (January 1954), 233-235, A. L. Bennett reports a study of the reading of three groups of college freshmen to determine the merits of (1) free reading, (2) regular instruction in outlining and précis writing, and (3) reading for meaning and getting the main point. The results of the study have implications for the person who is weighing the merits of different approaches to the guidance of reading. You may wish to review these.

9. In her book *Communication, the Miracle of Shared Living*, Dora V. Smith suggests that there is a fundamental relationship between the ability to communicate and the basic processes of our way of life in a democracy. What purposes for reading does she believe essential and what means does she suggest for their achievement?

OTHER SUGGESTED READINGS

Adams, Fay and others. *Teaching Children to Read.* New York: Ronald Press, 1949.

Association for Childhood Education International. *Adventuring in Literature with Children,* Bulletin No. 92. Washington, D.C.: Association for Childhood Education International, 1953.

Burger, I. Victor and others. *Bringing Children and Books Together.* New York: Library Clubs of America Inc., 1957.

Burton, William H. *The Guidance of Learning Activities.* New York: Appleton-Century-Crofts Co., 1952.

Children's Book Council. *The World of Children's Books.* New York: Children's Book Council, 1952.

Conference on Reading. University of Chicago, 1956. *Developing Permanent Interest in Reading;* compiled and edited by Helen M. Robinson. Supplementary Educational Monographs, No. 84. Chicago: University of Chicago Press, 1956.

Dent, Charles H. *Bulletin Boards for Teaching.* Austin: University of Texas, 1955.

Dolch, Edward W. *Methods in Reading.* Champaign, Ill. Garrard Press, 1955.

Donaldson, Beverly. "The Role of the Elementary Library in the Human Relations Program." Unpublished Master's essay. College of Education. Wayne University, Detroit, 1955.

Duff, Annis. *Longer Flight.* New York: Viking Press, 1955.

Fargo, Lucille F. *Activity Book for School Libraries.* Chicago: American Library Association, 1938.

Fargo, Lucille F. *Activity Book* (Library Projects for Children and Youth). Chicago: American Library Association, 1945.

Fenner, Phyllis. *Our Library.* New York: John Day Co., 1942.

Frank, Josette. *Your Child's Reading Today.* Garden City: Doubleday & Co., 1954.

Gates, Doris. *Helping Children Discover Books.* Chicago: Science Research Associates, 1956.

Grambs, Jean D. *Development of Lifetime Reading Habits.* New York: R. R. Bowker Co., 1954.

Gray, William S., ed. *Keeping Reading Programs Abreast of the Times:* Proceedings of the Annual Conference on Reading. Chicago: University of Chicago Press, 1950.

Hester, Kathleen B. *Teaching Every Child to Read.* New York: Harper & Brothers, 1955.

Lorang, Sister Mary Corde. *The Effect of Reading on Moral Conduct and Emotional Experience.* Washington, D.C.: Catholic University of America Press, 1945.

Michaelis, John U. *Social Studies for Children in a Democracy.* 2d ed. New York: Prentice-Hall, 1956.

Munson, Amelia H. *An Ample Field.* Chicago: American Library Association, 1950.

National Council of Teachers of English, Commission on the English Curriculum. *The English Language Arts.* New York: Appleton-Century-Crofts Co., 1952.

National Society for the Study of Education. *Reading in High School and College.* Forty-seventh Yearbook, Part 2. Chicago: University of Chicago Press, 1949.

New York State. Bureau of Secondary Curriculum Development. *The Road to Better Reading.* Albany, N.Y. State Department of Education, 1953.

Quiller-Couch, Arthur Thomas. *On the Art of Reading.* New York: G. P. Putnam's Sons, 1920.

"Reading for Today's Children." *National Elementary Principal.* Thirty-fourth Yearbook, XXV (September 1955).

Shaftel, George and Shaftel, Fannie R. *Role Playing the Problem Story.* New York: National Conference of Christians and Jews, 1952.

Smith, Dora V. *Communication, the Miracle of Shared Living.* New York: Macmillan Co., 1955.

Smith, Lillian H. *The Unreluctant Years.* Chicago: The American Library Association, 1953.

CHAPTER 7

READING FOR INFORMATION
AND KNOWLEDGE

*A knowledge of how to acquire knowledge is a permanent
possession which can be used throughout life.*
—CHARLES A. BEARD

Four-year-old Johnny is full of "satiable curiosity." Day
by day he directs to anyone who will listen a barrage of questions. What is it? Can I try it? What makes it go? Why is it
that way? How does it work? What do you do with it? Why do
you do that? And if understanding adults help him to find
answers, he learns fast.

When Johnny goes to school he continues to ask questions
and to search for answers as teachers provide experiences that
enlarge his world, that build bridges to new interests, that promote the identification of problems. Thus does Johnny start the
long thrust and drive to learn what the past has learned, and to
bring it to bear on his own concerns and relationships.

The extent to which he succeeds will depend largely on his
skill in "finding the facts, filtering the facts, facing the facts,
and following the facts." Carried to a logical conclusion, this
means that the *process*, the *how*, of the learning, is as important
as what is to be learned, and the teaching of the learning skills
as essential as teaching the facts.

What are the learning skills? How may they be identified?
Defined broadly, the term includes all the motor, computation,
communication, and interaction skills. All are means and procedures used in learning. The man on the street thinks of them as
"know-how." Defined more strictly the term denotes the skills
required in receiving and communicating ideas. Skill in reading,
observing, interviewing, telling, reporting, discussing, demonstrating, planning, and problem-solving are all procedures for

gathering and utilizing information and knowledge. They involve content as well as process, "since they are procedures for making understandings operative." [1] They are not easily learned apart from real situations. Neither are they learned by chance or by repetitive drill. They must be taught deliberately and practiced thoughtfully.

Skill in reading involves a wide variety of skills depending on the individual's purpose in reading. *Reading for information* makes certain specific skill demands on the reader. For example, *to locate information* the indiviual needs to identify and understand the meaning of words and have facility in using library aids and tools such as indexes, catalogs, and directories in locating desired information. *To select and organize information* he needs to develop skill in choosing significant ideas, identifying topic sentences, skimming, outlining, and note-taking. *Interpreting information* requires that he have skill in seeing cause and effect relationships, in judging the authoritativeness of sources, and in evaluating information on the basis of some of the values he holds; and, finally, *to utilize information* he needs to generalize and draw conclusions, to relate the facts to other situations. This, particularly, is a crucial step, for on it depends the degree to which the acquisition of information and knowledge affects the individual's values and beliefs and, in turn, his behavior.

With due consideration for the importance of all the learning skills, discussion on subsequent pages will be limited to the intermediate skills and understandings required in using the medium of print to bring knowledge to bear on the myriad of problems, relationships, and activities which the individual pursues throughout his life.

CONVENTIONAL PROGRAMS FOR TEACHING THE SKILLS

Heavy emphasis is placed on the communication skills in the public schools. In the primary grades a considerable share of the child's school day is spent in learning to read. In the

[1] W. H. Burton, "Implications for Organization of Instruction and Instructional Adjuncts," in *Learning and Instruction.* Forty-ninth Yearbook of the National Society for the Study of Education, Part I. (Chicago: University of Chicago Press, 1950), p. 246.

middle grades, teaching is directed towards reading for meaning, and efforts are made to teach the work-study skills, including the use of the dictionary, the encyclopedias, and other reference books. Pupils learn how books are arranged in the library and how they may be located by means of the card catalog. Many of the textbooks used by junior high school pupils contain chapters on the use of books and libraries. Teachers give assignments from these chapters and pupils work on them in the library.

In the high school grades many teachers use methods of class instruction that require pupils to locate, select, organize, and interpret information. Excellent as this procedure is, it breaks down when teachers assume that pupils already possess the required skills and need no further instruction. The chances are that reteaching of these skills needs to be done.

In high school English classes countless hours are spent in reading for interpretation and appreciation. Some instruction is given in outlining and note-taking. There is, at present, heavy emphasis in social studies texts on reading skills and critical thinking.

School librarians teach the use of books and libraries, relating the instruction to classroom assignments whenever it is possible to do so. Since skills are not learned effectively apart from real situations or in advance of need or meaning, results are not always encouraging.

In a midwestern city the Iowa Test of Work-Study Skills was given to some eleven hundred eighth-grade pupils in two large junior high schools. The test purports to evaluate the pupil's ability to use encyclopedias, dictionaries, indexes, and other general reference books, and to read maps, charts, and graphs. According to the author's norms, the pupils taking the test were retarded from one to three and a half grades. Yet an overwhelming majority of the pupils had attended elementary schools where for six years, twice each week, they had been regularly scheduled to the school library for directed reading and for instruction in the use of books and libraries.

Should one assume that this reflects on the teaching ability of the school librarian? Not at all. Classroom instruction in the elementary schools of that city was, in the main, subject-centered. Textbooks and workbooks were the major tools of instruction, and question-and-answer recitation the typical classroom procedure. The school library was regarded as a separate subject, a place where pupils were scheduled to go to read. The librarian taught the work-study skills, but the pupils had little need or chance to utilize and practice the skills. Hence they had not gained the facility in the use of books and libraries that might have been anticipated.

In spite of the heavy emphasis in the nation's schools on skill development, there is an uneasy feeling on the part of school and lay people alike that many pupils cannot read skillfully, use information expertly, or think critically.

Difficulties and Blocks

There are, without doubt, many reasons why this situation exists, the major one being that the skills are complex and not easily mastered. Other reasons may be cited.

1. In many schools low priority is placed on the teaching of these skills. Instruction tends to be incidental and sporadic and dependent upon the interest and skill of the teacher. Many teachers assume that English teachers and school librarians should give the instruction. Moreover, they find it difficult to teach the skills because they themselves have little facility in the methods of inquiry. They do not know sources and materials. They assign topics for pupils to "look up" in the library and tell pupils to use the encyclopedias. The attempts of the school librarian to have pupils use a variety of materials are often thwarted because pupils are interested only in securing the information that they think the teacher wants.

"Yes," said a twelfth-grade boy in reply to the librarian's suggestion that he get his information about Oliver Wendell Holmes from Bowen's *Yankee from Olympus*,[2] "the book looks good, but Miss Johnston wants us to get our material out of the

[2] Catherine Bowen, *Yankee from Olympus: Justice Holmes and His Family* (Boston: Little, Brown & Co., 1944).

encyclopedia." He proceeded to copy the biographical sketch of Holmes word for word from the encyclopedia. It is doubtful if such assignments are more than "gestures towards enriching classroom instruction."

Even in situations in which teachers conduct their classes so that pupils have considerable practice in selecting and utilizing information and in generalizing and drawing conclusions, they seldom help pupils to identify and understand the logical steps in the process. Hence pupils are unable to use the skills in other situations because teachers do not teach for transfer. They contrive a good environment for teaching these skills, but they fail to teach them. Useful as these skills are as classroom methods, they must be raised to the status of a major goal of teaching, a *what*, not just a *how*, in education.

2. Major responsibility for teaching the skills is often assigned to the school librarian, who cannot be expected to carry the teaching load. The school librarian gives much individual, incidental instruction as he works with boys and girls in the library. He explains the use of the card catalog a countless number of times a day. He helps pupils choose and organize information instead of copying it word for word from reference books. He demonstrates the use of the *Readers' Guide* and reminds pupils to use the index instead of the table of contents in searching for a specific subject in a book. Meaningful as such teaching is, it reaches only those pupils who come to the library.

When the librarian organizes a formal program of instruction and attempts to reach all the pupils in the school, he finds it difficult to plan on the basis of immediate needs and concerns of pupils and more difficult to provide adequate practice following the instruction. If he follows too rigidly some of the published instructional materials that present detailed lessons and assignments as if knowledge about such library tools was an "ultimate good," the learning is not very effective. School librarians need to initiate, encourage, and share in any or all skill development programs, but they should not expect to carry the major share of the instruction.

3. Conflicting opinions among a school staff about how knowledge is to be acquired and for what purposes block a concerted effort in the teaching of the communication and learning skills.

When members of a faculty believe that information, knowledge, and wisdom are synonymous; when they believe that the major purpose of the school is to present to children through the medium of textbooks a body of knowledge selected and organized by adults who have decided what particular information is important; when they act on the assumption that the most effective classroom procedure is assign, memorize, recite, test— then it follows that there will be little need for the pupils to understand and to practice the learning skills.

The above factors are serious blocks to improvement, since they involve the educational philosophy as well as the skills of teachers and librarians. Real improvement comes as teachers themselves become more skilled in the methods of inquiry, and as they implement in classroom practice the research findings on how children learn. From available evidence one may assume that when the concerns and needs of the child are considered, when his purposes are marshaled, when he sees some use for the information, then the required skills can be taught and practiced and information and knowledge brought to bear more effectively on the solution of problems, on decision-making, and on the development of understandings and values. The fact that many teachers and librarians are concerned about these skills and aware that improvement is possible and desirable makes the outlook promising.

ORGANIZING FOR TEACHING THE "LEARNING SKILLS"

When one is confronted with the task of developing a program for teaching the skills, one ponders such questions as these: What are the skills that the pupils should master? What skills are most crucial to his learning? When, where, and how shall they be taught? By whom? With what basic assumptions shall a program be initiated? On subsequent pages, these questions will be discussed.

On What Assumptions Shall a Program Be Based?

Members of school staffs who have participated in cooperative planning of skill development programs have found it helpful to start with some general agreements or assumptions about a program. These become bench marks or a frame of reference for the plans and projects that follow. The following appear to be important to the success of a program:

1. The teaching of the learning skills is done most effectively within a planned program that takes into strict account the need to teach the skills within the context of subject matter at the time when pupils need the skills in order *to locate and utilize information and knowledge.*

2. Since the learning of one skill often depends upon previous mastery of another, some kind of sequential order is required. For example, a child who has not learned the arrangement of the letters of the aphabet is handicapped in using the dictionary. Yet to define an exact sequential order for teaching the skills is a denial of the idea that a person learns a skill best in relation to content.

3. A skill is seldom learned in one try. Therefore, what is needed is considerable duplication and repetition in the teaching of these skills, a fact which may be considered advantageous. For example, take the skills involved in selecting and organizing information. One teacher may teach his class how to outline a chapter in a social studies textbook. Pupils may understand the steps involved, but it is doubtful that they will have acquired real facility in selecting and organizing information. Only when all teachers of the content subjects promote the process persistently in a variety of learning situations will pupils become habituated to the procedures to the point that they have acquired the skills.

4. The skills involved in reading for information and knowledge do not operate solely in the reading of non-fiction books

or other strictly informational material. The pupil can be taught
to select, organize, interpret, and evaluate information as he reads
fiction.   These are procedures or steps in the thinking process, an
activity as essential in reading fiction as in reading non-fiction.

When Shall They Be Taught?

The teaching of the skills needs to continue from grades one
through twelve. Since reading for understanding becomes increasingly complex as a child continues in school and since there are
a number of supplementary skills required for reading different
kinds of materials, the skills should be taught at the time they
are needed and retaught grade by grade.

This should not be taken to mean that a school staff can
identify the skills required and develop a series of lessons in
which grade levels are fixed. A staff whose members believe that
the skills are taught best in relation to subject matter within a
curriculum geared to the needs, life problems, or developmental
tasks of pupils would find it difficult, if not impossible, to organize
a formal program or devise strict time schedules.

On the other hand, they must structure flexible, vertical
programs to insure reaching every pupil and to provide for continuity and sequence in skill development. Many of these skills
should be taught at different levels of complexity, with an introduction in the lower grades, review and reteaching in later elementary grades, and the introduction of the more complicated
aspects of the skill in the high school.

For example, teaching the Dewey Decimal Classification
and the arrangement of books on the library shelves begins in the
first grade when children learn that picture books and easy fiction
are shelved together in the library. Grade by grade, as they read
more widely, they are taught how to locate other books in the
library by examining the shelf headings. During the middle and
upper grades pupils will need to locate and use diversified kinds
of books, and it is then that they will learn how books are classified and arranged by number on the library shelves.

Moreover, on the learning of some skills depends the individual's readiness to learn others. As noted previously, the pupil who has not learned the arrangement of the letters of the alphabet has considerable difficulty learning to use dictionaries, encyclopedias and indexes. This does not mean that the upper-grade teacher can take it for granted that all his pupils have acquired facility in alphabetizing and in locating books on the library shelves. The teacher must start where the individual is, not from some preconceived starting point held in common with others.

It is these factors that make it essential for a school staff to plan a program in which all the skills are identified with sequential steps indicated on a continuum or developmental basis.

Who Shall Teach These Skills?

Implicit in the preceding paragraphs is the answer to the question, who shall teach these skills? Every teacher is a skills teacher. Four steps are indicated for the classroom teacher as he plans skill development programs: (1) He formulates in broad outline the learnings he wants and expects to provide for his pupils; (2) he examines materials and resources; (3) using simple checklists and other evaluative techniques he discovers the skills his pupils already have acquired; and (4) with careful consideration of the above factors, he identifies and teaches the skills required by his pupils to read skillfully and to utilize information.

In social studies, for example, pupils need skill in reading charts and maps and in reading to understand the chronology of events and cause and effect relationships. In science and mathematics they must learn to read directions, to pursue logical steps in solving problems. In English classes pupils read to interpret, generalize, evaluate.

The librarian should be well qualified to participate with the teachers in the initial planning of units of study, in the selection of materials and resources, and in teaching the skills required for the effective use of the materials. Together, the teacher and

librarian will arrange schedules and provide pupils ample opportunity for learning and practicing the skills.

If every classroom teacher pursued this plan, would there be
too much repetition of instruction? Not at all. If the school
provides for continuous evaluation of work-study skills, the teacher will know where his pupils stand in the development of the
skills and what instruction is needed. The consideration of crucial
importance is that each member of a school staff provide a flexible
program of skill development on the basis of the needs of his
pupils, and not leave the instruction to chance or to the hurried,
incidental teaching of the school librarian.

What Skills Are to Be Taught?

The specific skills identified in this chapter are those required of the individual in locating and utilizing information—
in learning how to learn from print. Because of their number and
interrelatedness, they are considered under four skill areas that
suggest procedural steps for teaching them. These are: skills for
locating information, skills for selecting and organizing information, skills for analyzing and interpreting information, and skills
for utilizing information.

LOCATING INFORMATION

To gain facility in locating information, the individual needs
to master a number of intermediate skills—skills in using library
tools, reference books, and other printed materials as sources of
information and knowledge.

In the primary grades only the ground work can be laid for
developing these skills. Yet these foundations need to be solid
if mastery of more complex skills is to be realized.

The Primary Grades

While primary school children are taking their first steps
in learning to read, they are also gaining facility in such related
skills as learning the arrangement of the letters of the alphabet,

the parts of a book, and the location of picture books and easy fiction on library shelves. Some of these experiences are provided by the teacher, some by the school librarian. Both work with children to promote the development of alphabet skills, since these skills are fundamental to achievement in spelling and reading, and equally essential to the skillful use of indexes, dictionaries, directories, the telephone book, and other library tools. As young children have carefully planned experiences with books in the school library, as they handle and look at them, they gain acquaintance with the title page, the table of contents, and the index. They learn to locate a few books on the library shelves. They identify the symbols on the backs of books that help them to locate and return books to the shelves. Their first contacts with non-fiction works indicate to them that books are sources of information as well as "bequests of wings."

Thus do school librarians and primary teachers provide the experiential background, the readiness to learn the more complicated skills required in locating, finding, and gaining information from the printed page. The orderly procedure for the deliberate teaching of "the location skills" is under way.

The Intermediate Grades

By the time the child is nine or ten years old, he is exploring an ever-widening world, still recklessly curious, still seeking answers as he observes, inspects, listens, plays, and lives inside and outside the school. To locate and gather information at this stage of his development he needs to use a variety of source materials—books, magazines, pamphlets, audio-visuals—and he needs to learn how to locate them. Provision needs to be made, therefore, in the middle grades for teaching a number of library and learning skills. These include:

1. Learning about all the resources of a library.
2. Locating books on library shelves and learning about the general arrangement of libraries.
3. Understanding and using the Dewey Classification scheme.

4. Learning how to use the card catalog to locate books on the shelves.

5. Locating and learning the arrangement of picture and pamphlet files and other audio-visual materials in the library.

6. Learning how to find material in magazines through the use of the *Readers' Guide to Periodical Literature* and other indexes.

7. Learning how to use library tools and reference books such as encyclopedias and the *World Almanac* to locate desired information.

8. Learning how to use all parts of a book to locate information—the index, graphs, maps, charts, appendix, and illustrations.

The High School Grades

The pupil must acquire increased facility in locating information throughout the high school grades as he uses more diverse and difficult materials. He will learn how to use special reference books, handbooks, directories, and indexes to help him find the facts. The teacher and the school librarian will present and demonstrate the use of these tools as sources of ready information and as guides for locating other sources.

The high school librarian, in his day by day contacts with pupils in the library, will do a considerable amount of skill teaching as pupils bring reference requests to him. A word of caution is suggested. He should avoid spoon-feeding pupils. Although it is less time-consuming for him to locate reference materials himself, he needs to take the energy and time required to show the pupil how to find the desired information. The librarian's patience is taxed by the young people who "cannot find the book," although it stands expectantly in front of their eyes on the shelves, and by those who, with the book in hand, pursue the elusive special topic via the table of contents. Yet the librarian must resist the temptation to do the work for them.

When pupils have acquired considerable facility in locating materials in the library, other difficulties beset them. The librarian blessed with a sense of humor is secretly amused by dozens of incidents that occur daily because pupils have not yet developed judgment in deciding where materials may logically be found. There is the boy who is disgruntled because he "can't find Benjamin Franklin in *Current Biography*," and the girl who searches diligently for Chaucer in *Twentieth Century Authors*.

The librarian reteaches the skills a hundred times a day on the assumption that pupils do not master a skill at one trial but may do so eventually if they get enough practice under insightful supervision.

The skills for locating information that should be taught in the high school grades include:

1. Locating books on library shelves (understanding the Dewey Classification scheme).

2. Learning to use the card catalog to locate materials in the library.

3. Learning to use a number of special reference books in different subject fields—history, biography, literature, music, art, social sciences, science.

4. Learning to use magazine indexes, such as the *Readers' Guide to Periodical Literature* and other specialized indexes, as sources for locating current materials.

5. Learning to use all parts of the book: the title page, preface, introduction, table of contents, lists of maps and illustrations, notes, appendix, bibliography and glossary.

6. Learning to use dictionaries, encyclopedias, annuals, almanacs, yearbooks, atlases and maps.

7. Learning to use special indexes—poetry, plays, costumes, essays, songs and biography—to find materials in collections.

8. Learning to use handbooks, manuals, directories and yearbooks for locating all kinds of useful information.

Selecting and Organizing Information

If pupils do not know how to organize knowledge in some logical fashion which expedites learning, they have no alternative but to try to memorize information. This is a time-consuming performance, and the rate of forgetting is high. Inability to select the facts is an even greater handicap, for this means that the person who does not select facts pertinent to the problem may come out with a completely erroneous set of conclusions from the facts at hand.

Pupils therefore need continuous help and guidance in developing facility in these two closely related skills, selecting and organizing information. Observation of boys and girls as they read informational materials, take notes, and give reports in classes provides evidence to indicate that these skills need to be taught deliberately and directly. They are not acquired by chance.

The Elementary Grades

Reading teachers in the primary grades help pupils identify and understand the meaning of written concepts. This process involves the selection and organization of ideas at a very elementary level. In the middle grades, as pupils begin to read for information, the task of selecting and organizing ideas becomes more complicated and teachers and librarians alike need to follow some such orderly procedure in teaching the essential skills. Several suggestions provide direction for instruction:

1. Help pupils understand what the author is saying.

2. Teach them to look up the meaning of words in the dictionary.

3. Help pupils choose information that has particular use and meaning in relation to the purpose they have for reading. Since the individual's purpose for reading determines to a considerable degree what he selects, the teacher needs to help him identify what it is that he is trying to find out.

4. Help pupils select the most important ideas and facts and arrange them in some kind of logical order.

5. Help them arrange less important facts under the main headings, either in the form of notes or in outline form.

The teacher who watches the struggles of fourth graders writing their first compositions about an incident that happened to them, or about the life of a famous person, or about the story that has been read aloud to them, realizes with what care children have to be taught to select and organize information. It is a laborious step by step procedure, but the importance of the learning can hardly be overestimated.

The school librarian meets the problem face to face as ten- and eleven-year-olds begin to come to the library to "get reports" and to "look up information." She notes their tendency to copy "word for word," because they do not know how to select and organize.

If, at that time, outlining and note-taking are deliberately taught, the foundations are laid for good habits of study and for the mastery of the more complex skills required for reading at a higher level of comprehension.

The High School Grades

Regardless of the amount of emphasis given to skill development in the elementary school, the high school staff cannot assume that the pupils need no further guidance in selecting and organizing information. Instruction should continue throughout the high school grades with emphasis on the following intermediate skills:

1. Identifying the purposes for acquiring the information.

2. Skimming to ascertain if the selection contains information pertinent and relevant to the problem.

3. Choosing a number of important topics under which the information may be grouped.

4. Selecting and classifying less important facts under the main topics.

5. Examining large or major topics to determine the most systematic arrangement as it relates to the problem.

6. Selecting *all* the facts that *bear* on the problem.

7. Jotting down sources of information and looking up unfamiliar words.

One of the most effective methods for teaching these skills is demonstration. For example, in helping pupils understand the steps involved in selecting and organizing information, choose a selection that lends itself to a problem under discussion. Read it aloud to the group, sentence by sentence and paragraph by paragraph, stating what you believe is the central thought. You may ask yourself questions relating to what the author means to say, checking the information to ascertain if it is related and pertinent to the problem under discussion. Then begin to organize the information on the basis of main and subordinate ideas. The finished product may be either in the form of an outline or notes. The pupils will criticize and question and then try by themselves.

Point out to the pupils the importance of balanced and unbiased selection of the facts. Take, for example, any article on socialized medicine. The prejudiced person might select only information that dwelt on the advantages (or disadvantages), thereby furnishing a set of facts from which erroneous conclusions might be reached.

When students are gathering information that involves going to a number of sources, they will need instruction in other procedures, such as (1) keeping notes on separate slips of paper; (2) recording in bibliographical form the different sources of information—the author, title, publisher, and pages of the book or magazine on which information is found; and (3) combining and coordinating the information gained from several sources into one organized report.

If you are a high school librarian or if you are planning to be one, you may take a very dim view of your responsibility for the teaching of these skills, and indeed in many high schools the librarian has neither the time nor opportunity to do so. But no person in the school is more acutely aware of the problem. Day by day, high school librarians watch pupils copying information from printed materials, information that apparently has little meaning for them or slight usefulness other than "doing an assignment." Librarians are able to give some incidental instruction as they help students "do reference work" in the library, but they can hardly find the time to give the individualized guidance needed by every pupil who enters the library, as the following incident clearly demonstrates:

> In a high school in an urban area where pupils were retarded, on the average, three to four grades in reading and work-study skills, a ninth-grade class was studying the Middle Ages. The teacher sent a group to the library to get reports on a number of related topics. It fell to the lot of one boy to look up Charlemagne. The next day in class he gave his report. Pulling from his pocket a frayed piece of paper he began to read: "Charlemagne is the world's champion turncoat. One moment it is brilliant green; the next it may be a gray-black or crimson and black or covered with yellow spots."

It was evident that *Charlemagne* and *chameleon* stood close to one another in the encyclopedia. That the report had nothing to do with the Middle Ages disturbed the boy not at all. In selecting information, he had not said to himself, "Are the facts related to the problem?"

This is by no means a unique situation. Similar incidents occur over and over in schools where librarians cannot give incidental instruction to every pupil who comes to the library and where teachers take it for granted that pupils have previously acquired skill to read with understanding and to make a balanced selection of information on a subject or problem.

Analyzing and Interpreting Information

After the individual has *found* and *filtered* the facts, he must now *face* the facts—assuming that he has read, memorized, taken notes, or made an outline so that he has an organized record of what he has read. He now needs to analyze and interpret the information—to answer the question, what does the information mean?

There should be no inference that the skillful reader follows these procedural steps in a strict sequential order. He may organize information as he skims a page. He may interpret and evaluate as he organizes his facts. The process of selection inevitably involves him in some interpretation of the facts. It is even possible that he may shift his original purpose as he reads. Yet in learning to read skillfully, it is important that the individual pupil identify and pursue some orderly procedure until the intermediate skills are learned and he is habituated to their use.

The purpose of interpretation is to adapt information into a meaningful pattern which reveals pertinent relationships by which conclusions are reached. It is in this step that the values, attitudes, and purposes of the person making the interpretations are so influential because invariably he tends to harmonize these with the facts and information at hand.

If the interpreter is biased about a problem, the facts often are "all on his side." This is serious in that it may lead the interpreter to a completely erroneous set of conclusions, as the following incident illustrates:

A group of students entered the library to find information on the question, What is the nature of the flying saucers? After a thorough reading of many magazine articles on the subject, they reported back to class three different sets of conclusions: (1) flying saucers are hallucinations, (2) they are space ships from other planets, (3) they are instruments of warfare being tested by another nation.

The source of the information and the bias of the interpreter were reflected in the answers, when the obvious answer was that at that time there was not enough evidence to support any conclusion.

How do the teacher and the librarian teach youth to interpret and analyze information? A number of intermediate skills are basic to the interpretation of what is read:

1. Understanding what the author means.
2. Relating and evaluating pertinent ideas.
3. Evaluating the reliability of sources.

4.   Recognizing and analyzing propaganda.
5.   Distinguishing between fact and opinion.
6.   Noting sources, making footnotes and bibliographies.
7.   Indicating time and place sequences.
8.   Recognizing and tracing pertinent relationships.
9.   Evaluating one's own values as one examines data.

Demonstration by the teacher appears to be a good instructional technique. He may read a selection that brings information to bear on some problem of concern to the class. He will select and organize the information. Then, by adroit questioning, he will help the class to interpret and evaluate the information. He may ask:

1.   Have I selected and organized all the facts related and pertinent to the problem? Are recency and adequacy of the information important? Have social values changed since the information was reported?

2.   Do I understand all the ideas and concepts presented in the information? Are they *fact* or *opinion?* What is the difference between fact and opinion? If opinion, what are the author's values and biases? Can I rely on his integrity? Is the source reliable?

3.   Have I considered all the possible relationships in the *information,* such as time and place, cause and effect?

4.   How do I react to the information? Is the subject one about which I already hold strong opinions, and, if so, have I looked at all the evidence with an open mind?

Repeated demonstration by the teacher followed by demonstration and practice by pupils should result in increased facility in the interpretation of information. The high school youth who develops this skill will be able to detect and evaluate propaganda. When all the facts and issues are presented to him, one of democracy's choicest freedoms, the privilege of free inquiry, of making judgments on the basis of available evidence, will be within his reach.

Reaching Conclusions and Utilizing Information and Knowledge

If knowledge is to work for the individual so that it becomes the basis for his decisions and the touchstone of his values and beliefs, he must learn how to generalize and reach conclusions from the accumulated facts.

This should not be taken to mean that the individual must always "do something" with the facts or that he must immediately "act" on the conclusions. He has utilized knowledge when it gives him a fresh viewpoint, a different way of thinking or conjecturing about things. If he has generalized or made a value judgment on the basis of the information, if he reflects on the simple question, *What does this mean to me?*—then learning is taking place, and information and knowledge are being brought to bear on his values and beliefs and ultimately, it is hoped, on his behavior.

The Elementary Grades

The little child begins to utilize knowledge when he is brought face to face with cause and effect relationships. He is indeed fortunate if he has the constant guidance of a thoughtful, loving adult who helps him to generalize but not to go beyond the facts. Kindergarten teachers know how eagerly children evaluate new ideas and relate them to their own experiences. Librarians observe the insights that tiny pupils bring to the simplest stories and their ability to discriminate between right and wrong and see simple cause and effect relationships. This activity needs to be encouraged since it establishes the ground work for generalizing from information at a more complex level.

The following anecdote illustrates young children's readiness to apply what they have learned:

With amazement a mother observed her four-year-old carefully dropping pebbles as they walked to a nearby store. Just the night before Ann had listened with wide-eyed wonder to the story of Hop o' My Thumb, whose foresight in dropping pebbles as he and his brothers were led into the forest enabled them to find their way home. Ann was taking no chances.

She had drawn some conclusions from her reading, erroneous to be sure. She was, however, utilizing information.

But the process grows complicated and difficult, and teachers must not assume it is learned by chance.

In the middle grades the inventive teacher constantly helps his pupils to interpret information and reach conclusions to the end that they may refine their opinions and form judgments. He provides many opportunities for his pupils to report the facts and in addition to clarify and relate the facts to other situations. He asks questions: *how?* and *why?* and *what does this mean to me?* Thus he promotes the habit of reflection.

The High School Grades

As instruction continues in the high school grades, there are numerous questions that teachers may use to give direction for reaching generalizations and conclusions and for evaluating decisions:

1. What are the possible conclusions and generalizations which can be drawn from an analysis of the information?

2. Have you taken into account your own biases and prejudices which might have influenced the reaching of these conclusions?

3. Have you gone beyond your information in reaching conclusions?

4. What do your conclusions indicate? Have they changed or clarified any of your previously held opinions or judgments?

5. Can you use this information in making judgments and reaching decisions in other areas or with other problems?

6. May further information make necessary a possible reconsideration of conclusions?

It is the generalizing and concluding stage that reveals sharply the difference between the content- and problem-centered method of teaching. The above questions hardly apply to the strict question-

and-answer type of instruction in which the pupil studies a text and the teacher asks questions that elicit the recall of facts. As instruction moves away from question-and-answer recitation toward methods that promote the identification and solution of problems, the chances are increased for larger numbers of young people to acquire skill and facility in using knowledge in the solution of personal and social problems.

The research of the past twenty years seems to show that it is a fallacy to count on the transfer of training—on the transfer of knowledge and information to other situations—unless teachers deliberately teach for such transfer. If learning is to be useful, there should be many likenesses between the situation in which the learning is acquired and those in which it is to be used.

Studies in critical thinking show that ability to think and to gather and utilize information in one field does not of necessity bring ability to think clearly in other fields. The atomic scientist who would never draw conclusions in his own field except on the basis of controlled and verified experimentation has been known to make unwarranted generalizations in regard to social relationships. It seems fair to assume that pupils need many opportunities to generalize in many situations from all kinds of data.

Possibly the best evaluation of the effectiveness of the skill development program in the high school is suggested by Eugene Gaier in these two questions: "Can the student manipulate the facts he acquires and apply them to new situations? Can he attack a new problem by using certain generalized techniques as well as by utilizing learned information?" [3] It would seem that these questions strike at the heart of the problem. The individual who can reply to them in the affirmative has *skill* in utilizing information in the process of thinking. He can take the most serious problems and turn on them "the white light of reason." A school staff which encourages the development of these skills has done well.

[3] Eugene L. Gaier, "Knowledge in Problem Solving," *Progressive Education*, XXX (March 1953), 138-142.

IMPLICATIONS AND RECOMMENDATIONS

For school librarians who answer hundreds of reference questions, direct innumerable pupils to the sources of information, help them to use the tools more effectively—and for teachers who seek to provide more effective learning experiences for their pupils —the following implications and recommendations are offered:

1. Helping pupils to develop the learning skills calls for a high degree of understanding and skill on the part of teachers and librarians. It calls for the kind of classroom instruction that motivates the teaching of the skills. It calls for the same kind of deliberate teaching that is provided for the computation skills. Instruction should include the procedural steps in the process, namely: *finding, selecting, organizing, interpreting,* and *utilizing* information, as well as such intermediate skills as skimming, notetaking, outlining, reporting, discussing, and evaluating. Provision needs to be made for the continuous practice of these skills during which pupils have an opportunity to correct mistakes, ask questions, and receive individual assistance, since practice without guidance and continuous evaluation of progress is not effective.

2. The skills must be taught with due consideration of the maturity of the pupil at the time when the skill is essential and useful in the learning of the pupil. No carefully devised program can be followed grade by grade, yet some developmental line should be followed within a comprehensive, planned program to insure that the pupil learns the skills when he needs them.

3. The expenditure of the time and energy required to teach these skills appears worth while since statistically significant gains occur in the more mature types of interpretation and reasoning as a result of well designed developmental reading programs in the content fields.

4. If one of the major purposes of the public school in a democracy is to educate citizens who have the will and ability to solve the most serious problems through the process of thinking, then educators must be increasingly concerned that the products of the schools be not only literate, but that they have the ability to

think logically, critically, and dispassionately on the basis of collected evidence. It seems reasonable to assume that this will be achieved only by painstaking attention to the mastery of the "learning skills."

5. The development of skills, understandings, and values are inextricably related. If values are developed as the child meets many life situations and has an opportunity to generalize from them, if understandings are built on information and knowledge, and if skills are ways of making understandings operative, it follows that the school must provide the kinds of organized learning experiences for its pupils that promote the meshing of skills, understandings, and values into lasting habits of mind and heart.

Problems for Discussion and Study

1. What are the dictionary definitions of *information, knowledge, wisdom*? What is the relationship of information to learning? If learning is defined as a change in behavior, what teaching is required to help the child learn?

2. Assume that a fifth-grade class is scheduled to the library every week during the school year. Make a general plan for teaching the specific skills required for finding and utilizing information.

3. Many teachers appear to be more concerned about the "products of thought" than the "processes of thought." Attack or defend this statement by citing examples from your own experiences.

4. "Every teacher is a teacher of reading." Do you agree with this statement? Justify your position.

5. The statement is sometimes made that when students read skillfully there is little danger in exposing them to information on controversial subjects, even to subversive information and propaganda. Do you believe this? Defend your position.

6. Studies have revealed that the rate of forgetting of factual information is very high. Have you any suggestions as to how learning can be made more permanent by the improvement and application of the "learning skills"?

7. Why does it appear wise for the classroom teacher rather than for the school librarian to teach many of the work-study skills? What contribution should the librarian make to the teaching of the skills?

8. What might be a minimum program for teaching the skills in the elementary grades? In the high school?

9. Assume the statement below to be true. Justify the conclusion which you believe logically follows:

The present techniques used by librarians in giving library instruction discourage and impede the use of the library by pupils.

10. A considerable amount of research has been undertaken recently to study the relationships of reading and critical thinking. K. L. Husbands and J. H. Shores, in the *Journal of Educational Research*, XLIII (February 1950), 453-65, summarized a number of these studies and pointed to the need of further research designed to clarify these relationships. If you are interested in the implications of these studies, you may wish to review and summarize a number of them.

OTHER SUGGESTED READINGS

Bond, Guy L. and Bond, Eva. *Developmental Reading in High School.* New York: Macmillan Co., 1941.

Bond, Guy L. and Bond, Eva. *Child Growth in Reading.* Chicago: Lyons & Carnahan, 1955.

Bullock, Harrison. *Helping the Non-reading Pupil in the Secondary School.* New York: Bureau of Publications, Teachers College, Columbia University, 1956.

Cartwright, William H. *How to Use a Textbook.* How to Do It Series, No. 2. Washington, D.C.: National Council for the Social Studies, 1950.

Center, Stella S. *The Art of Book Reading.* New York: Charles Scribner's Sons, 1953.

Cronbach, Lee J., ed. *Text Materials in Modern Education.* Urbana: University of Illinois Press, 1955.

Cummings, Howard H. and Bard, Harry. *How to Use Daily Newspapers.* How to Do It Series, No. 5. Washington, D.C.: National Council for the Social Studies, 1949.

Dale, Edgar. *How to Read a Newspaper.* Chicago: Scott, Foresman & Co., 1941.

Grambs, Jean D. *Using Current Materials to Study Current Problems.* Stanford, Calif.: Stanford University Press, 1952.

Gray, William S., ed. *Improving Reading in All Curriculum Areas.* Proceedings of the Annual Conference on Reading. Chicago: University of Chicago Press, 1952.

Gray, William S., ed. *Promoting Growth Toward Maturity in Interpreting What Is Read.* Proceedings of the Annual Conference on Reading. Chicago: University of Chicago Press, 1951.

Gray, William S. and Rogers, Bernice. *Maturity in Reading.* Chicago: University of Chicago Press, 1956.

Harris, A. J. *How to Increase Reading Ability.* New York: Longmans, Green & Co., 1956.

Hester, Kathleen B. *Teaching Every Child to Read.* New York: Harper & Brothers, 1955.

Hummel, William and Huntress, Keith. *The Analysis of Propaganda.* New York: William Sloane Associates, 1949.

Jackson, Holbrook. *The Reading of Books.* New York: Charles Scribner's Sons, 1947.

Kinney, Lucien and Dresden, Katherine. *Better Learning Through Current Materials.* Stanford, Calif.: Stanford University Press, 1952.

McCullough, Constance M. *Problems in the Improvement of Reading.* New York: McGraw-Hill Book Co., 1955.

McKim, Margaret G. *Guiding Growth in Reading.* New York: Macmillan Co., 1955.

National Council for the Social Studies. *Skills in the Social Studies.* Edited by Helen McCracken Carpenter. Twenty-fourth Yearbook. Washington, D.C.: National Council for the Social Studies, 1954.

National Society for the Study of Education. *Learning and Instruction.* Forty-ninth Yearbook, Part 1. Chicago: University of Chicago Press, 1950.

Peterson, Eleanor M. *Aspects of Readability in the Social Studies.* New York: Bureau of Publications, Teachers College, Columbia University, 1954.

Russell, David H. *Children's Thinking.* Boston: Ginn & Co., 1956.

Simpson, Elizabeth. *Helping High School Students Read Better.* Chicago: Science Research Associates, 1954.

Strang, Ruth and Bracken, Dorothy Kendall. *Making Better Readers.* Boston: D. C. Heath & Co., 1957.

Triggs, Frances Orlind. *We All Teach Reading.* The Author, 419 W. 119th St., New York 27, 1954.

Walraven, Margaret Kessler, and Hall-Quest, A. L. *Library Guidance for Teachers.* New York: John Wiley and Sons, 1941.

Walraven, Margaret Kessler and Hall-Quest, A. L. *Teaching Through the Elementary School Library.* New York: H. W. Wilson Co., 1948.

Witty, Paul A. *Helping Children Read Better.* Chicago: Science Research Associates, 1950.

Yoakam, Gerald A. *Basal Reading Instruction.* New York: McGraw-Hill Book Co., 1955.

CHAPTER 8

PROCEDURES FOR TEACHING THE SKILLS

> What one knows is, in youth, of little moment; they know
> enough who know how to learn.
> —HENRY ADAMS

> Not the fact avails, but the use you make of it.
> —RALPH WALDO EMERSON

When members of a school staff accept the idea that teaching
the processes of thought may be as important as teaching the
products of thought, when they recognize their responsibility to
help youth use information and knowledge effectively, when they
identify the skills involved, they are confronted by such practical
problems as the following: What *are* the most important sources
of information, and how shall we teach pupils to use them?
What teaching aids and tools are available, and how shall we
evaluate pupil progress?

A number of answers to these questions can be suggested.

THE SOURCES OF INFORMATION AND KNOWLEDGE

Formal teacher education takes little note of this important
phase of curriculum development. The skills are discussed in
college classes as classroom methods rather than teaching content.
Reading efficiency and study-skills courses are offered as electives,
but many beginning teachers have only a cursory acquaintance
with sources and with library and research techniques. Often
they are unaware of the resources available to their pupils in
school and public libraries and are ill equipped to keep informed
about new learning materials that become available in ever growing numbers. With little facility in these skills, the teacher can
hardly be expected to give his pupils opportunity for mastering
them.

While these factors often block improvement in the learnings provided children in many schools, they yield to careful planning. The school librarian must play a crucial role in helping teachers gain facility in the use of library resources and materials and the skills necessary for helping their pupils to locate and utilize information. Librarians need to devise a variety of means to orient new teachers to library resources and to encourage all the teachers in a continuous study of books and other instructional materials and in their use with pupils. The teacher, also, needs to take some initiative in keeping in close touch with the library and the librarian.

A list indicating the minimum skill requirements is suggested for the teacher. If he can check a majority of the items in the affirmative, he is ready to promote like learnings with his pupils.

A Checklist for the Teacher

1. *Can you locate in your school and public library:*

Books in your own and in related fields
General reference books
Magazines—both current and bound copies
Clippings, pamphlet and picture files
Community resource files
Audio-visual materials—records, films, and filmstrips
Curriculum and teaching guides
College catalogs
Maps, travel guides, and posters
Vocational monographs and pamphlets
Professional books, magazines, and other literature in your
    own and related fields

2. *Do you know the general reference books—their scope. arrangement, and specific uses:*

General encyclopedias—both children's and adult
Dictionaries, word books, and usage books
Handbooks—curiosity, literary, historical, and statistical

Yearbooks, almanacs, and other records of progress
Biographical dictionaries—both current and historical
Gazetteers, atlases, globes, guide books
Manuals, directories—governmental and industrial
Special cyclopedias in your own field—music, art, literature,
    or science

3. *Are you acquainted with sources and can you use indexes
and guides to locate library materials:*

Indexes to materials in magazines and newspapers
        The Readers' Guide to Periodical Literature
        The Education Index
Indexes to audio-visual materials
        Film and filmstrip guides
        Indexes to pictures, records, recordings
Lists of free and inexpensive learning and curriculum ma-
    terials
        The Vertical File Index and other authoritative lists
Indexes to literature in collections
        Poetry, biography, essays, short stories, plays,
            fairy tales, and costumes
Subject lists of books and other instructional materials
        Vocational and historical fiction
        Subject indexes for primary, intermediate, and
            high school readers
        Lists provided in resource units and curriculum
            guides
        Lists for reluctant readers

4. *Do you follow a planned program for keeping in close
touch with new books and new instructional materials by methodi-
cal procedures:*

Examining authoritative lists and bibliographies
Reading book reviewing periodicals
Examining and evaluating new materials
Visiting the library regularly

*5. Are you skillful in searching for materials by the follow-
ing means:*

Using the Dewey Classification system
Locating books by using the card catalog
Using effective procedures in library searching
Selecting the best reference books for a given problem
Taking effective notes and developing a bibliography
Reading, evaluating, and interpreting information efficiently

*6. Are you familiar with the many available aids and tools
for teaching library and work-study skills:*

Chapters in textbooks devoted to the use of the library and
the learning skills
Curriculum guides and manuals on the use of the library [1]
Films and filmstrips on the use of reference books and other
library tools [2]

The teacher who makes a painstaking effort to increase his
own skills and who depends on the school librarian to cooperate
in the undertaking will find himself well equipped to teach his
pupils the skills required for locating, organizing, evaluating,
and utilizing information.

A FRAMEWORK FOR TEACHING THE SKILLS

True as it is that librarians and teachers must plan for teaching the skills with painstaking attention to the needs and developmental tasks of their own pupils and the demands of the curriculum, a summary of suggestions and procedures may provide general direction. Graphically presented on subsequent pages, the
lists of *Desirable Learnings for Pupils* indicate the purpose and
intent of the *Action Recommendations for Teachers and Librarians.*

[1] See the list of Suggested Aids and Tools at the end of this chapter.
[2] Among available filmstrips on the work-study skills are the following: "Library
Tools Series," by Young America; "Use Your Library," by the American Library
Association and the Society for Visual Education; "How to Read Series," by the
Society of Visual Education; "Learning to Study Series," by the Jam Handy Organization; "Basic Library Methods Series," by the Society of Visual Education;
and "Our Library," by Encyclopaedia Britannica Films.

Some explanation of how the charts might be used appears appropriate. Suggesting a specific program for promoting appreciation and interest in reading and the development of the requisite skills would be a rejection of what is known about effective teaching and learning.

Moreover, the mastery of special skills such as the use of the card catalog is only one aspect of skill development. Current trends in curriculum development require a broad approach to the teaching of understandings and skills. The wisdom of having the teacher and librarian provide for the integration of knowledge, appreciations, understandings, and skills in specific learning situations suggests the need for comprehensive guides and aids.

The charts are presented to give an *overview* of the understandings, appreciations, and skills that appear crucial in the learning of children and youth. The teacher and librarian will choose from the lists the specific learning objectives, procedures, and materials that *in combination,* and with constant appraisal of the needs of a particular group of pupils, and the content of the curriculum, may provide for continuity and integration of instruction.

CHART 1. GETTING ACQUAINTED WITH THE SOURCES OF INFORMATION

Desirable Learnings for Pupils	Action Recommendations for Teachers and Librarians
1. Understanding the many and varied sources of information.	1.(a) Pupil-teacher discussion of the sources of information—people, museums, galleries, libraries, radio, TV, records and recordings, pictures, institutions and organizations, movies, book and non-book printed materials.
	(b) Arranging visits and field trips to the public library, museums, organizations, institutions, and agencies.
2. Understanding what skills are involved in locating and using information.	2.(a) Pupil-teacher discussion of the various ways of gathering information and knowledge—listening, looking, hearing, smelling, experiencing, reading, interviewing, going to see.
	(b) Use of checklists, questions, and study forms to test students' awareness of things close at hand—their ability to listen, to observe, to appreciate.
3. Getting acquainted with the school library as one important source of information.	3.(a) Planning of schedules to insure all pupils regular library experiences.
	(b) Orienting all new pupils to the school library.
	(c) Arranging for library tours which include the location, examination, and explanation of all library resources and tools—books, magazines, pictures, pamphlets, and other audio-visual resources.
	(d) Explanation to all pupils about essential regulations governing library circulation, library schedules, and the effective use of library resources.

4. Developing wholesome attitudes and habits in using the library—to explore, to browse, to pursue hobbies and interests, to find answers to questions and problems.

4.(a) Provision of time, motivation, and organization to make it possible for pupils to use the school library.

(b) Developing an environment in the library that encourages reading, browsing, and searching for information.

(c) Providing classroom instruction and teaching methods that motivate inquiry and promote the use of many and various sources of information.

CHART 2. LEARNING HOW TO USE AND ENJOY BOOKS

Desirable Learnings for Pupils

1. An understanding of and belief in the importance of the book as a source of information, and a record of the cultural heritage of man's imagination and his best ideas.

2. Knowledge about how a book is written, illustrated, published, printed, distributed. Appreciation of authorship and of fine books and book-making.

Action Recommendations for Teachers and Librarians

1. (a) Provision for all pupils to handle books, to look at displays and exhibits of books, to pursue individual interests, to gain acquaintance with many books.

(b) Provision of time to read, provision for book discussions, for individual and group guidance of reading, for keeping reading records.

(c) Demonstrations and instruction in the care and handling of books.

(d) Discussion with mature pupils about the history of books and printing, the growth of libraries and great book collections.

(e) Discussion and study of such problems as the freedom of the press, censorship, book burning, and the place of books in a democracy.

2. (a) Teacher-pupil discussion of how books are written and published. Questions like the following are useful: Do you read and select books by the same author? How can you find out about your favorite author? Why are books dedicated? What information is found on the title page? When is the copyright date important? What purposes do illustrations fulfill?

(b) Enlisting and encouraging class discussion of first editions, rare books, literary forgeries, book collecting, association copies, literary prizes and awards, book clubs.

(c) Provision for the participation of pupils in planning and arranging displays and exhibits of fine books, of autographs and book dedications, illustrations from books, and pictures of authors.

(d) Provision for pupils to interview authors, to help plan book fairs, to arrange for speakers about books, to discuss TV programs featuring books and authors.

(e) Arranging field trips to printing and newspaper plants, book stores, public and private libraries to see special collections.

3. Knowledge of and skill in the use of the special features of a book.	3.(a) Identification and explanation of the use of the following special features in a book: the table of contents, index, list of illustrations, maps and charts, graphs, illustrations, appendix, preface and introduction. Instruction will emphasize the arrangement, purposes and use of these features with special emphasis on the use of the index in locating a subject or specific topic in the book and the way it differs from the table of contents.
	(b) Pupil-teacher discussion on how to use a textbook. One of the pamphlets in the *How To Do It Series* published by the National Council for the Social Studies gives helpful hints for teaching.
4. Understanding the value of the charts and graphs in non-fiction and facility in their use.	4.(a) Instruction in using charts including such aspects as: the value and use of different kinds of charts—time tables, flow charts (family trees), comparison charts, and pictorial charts—and the value of charts showing relationships and comparisons.
	(b) Pupil-teacher discussion of the kinds of information gained in the skillful reading of graphs. Points to be emphasized include: the use of graphs to illustrate changes and differences; the use of bar graphs to illustrate quantitative differences such as differences in temperature; the use of a pie or circle graph to illustrate relative percentage of the whole (such as the portion of the national income or money spent on soft drinks); the use of picture symbols to show comparisons.
5. Understanding how to read maps and use atlases.	5.(a) Instruction in map reading to include: using the index or lists of maps in atlases to locate the required map; using the grid lines to locate specific places on the map; noting the scale of a map and computing distance; identifying symbols and legends; using different kinds of maps such as: physical, commercial, economic, historical, political, outline, and air-age maps.
	(b) Examination and study of atlases, their arrangement, scope, and use.
6. Appreciating, enjoying, using book illustrations.	6.(a) Pupil-teacher discussion of the illustrations in fiction and non-fiction—their values and uses.
	(b) Opportunity to examine and talk about pictures in books. Judging their effectiveness by using such questions as: Is the picture stimulating, significant, relevant, authentic, artistic, properly colored? Do you like it? Why?
	(c) Introduction of outstanding illustrators and their books.

CHART 3. LOCATING BOOKS AND AUDIO-VISUAL MATERIALS IN THE LIBRARY

Desirable Learnings for Pupils	*Action Recommendations for Teachers and Librarians*
1. Understanding of the varied purposes and opportunities in acquiring and utilizing knowledge through the skillful use of books.	1. (a) Introduction and discussion by both teachers and librarians of many books appropriate to pupils' present and potential interests and needs, as well as appropriate books for classroom undertakings.
	(b) Using books to find specific information, to read for a variety of purposes.
	(c) Teacher-pupil discussion of the different fields of knowledge.
2. Knowledge of how books are arranged in most libraries.	2. (a) Explanation and demonstration of the use of shelf headings in locating books in a library.
	(b) Explanation and demonstration of the general arrangement of books in a library: the subject arrangement of non-fiction works; the arrangement of fiction alphabetically by author; the special arrangement of biography, reference books, and other special collections.
3. Acquaintance with and facility in using the Dewey classification scheme to locate books in the library.	3. (a) Explanation and discussion of the Dewey Decimal System of classification, with emphasis on such points as: its origin and history; the ten general subject or class divisions; the smaller divisions and more minute subdivisions; the assignment of numbers to these groupings; the call number of books; the arrangement of books by call numbers on the shelves.
	(b) Practice in locating and shelving books by classification number.

4. **Skill in the use of the card catalog for locating books on library shelves.**

    4. (a) Explanation and discussion of the arrangement and use of the catalog as a tool in locating books on library shelves. Instruction will emphasize such points as: the alphabetical arrangement of the cards in the catalog; the representation of the book under its author, title, or subjects in the catalog; the placement of the classification number of the book on each card, thereby providing for locating the book on the shelf; the advantages of listing books in the catalog under the subject as well as by author and title; the use of "see" and "see also" references.

    (b) Provision for pupils to find books on the shelves by looking up a book in the catalog by its title, and by its author, and by looking for books on a given subject in the card catalog and locating them on the shelves. Continued practice under guidance.

5. **The ability to use guides and indexes in locating films, filmstrips, records, and other audio-visual materials—those available in the school and those available through other agencies.**

    5. (a) Instruction, demonstration and practice in the use of appropriate guides and indexes to audio-visual materials, emphasizing the frequency of publication, scope, arrangement, and cumulation.

    (b) Practice and use of these guides in locating records, pictures, filmstrips, for classroom activities and units of work.

    (c) Instruction and practice in locating audio-visual materials that are housed and organized in the school library. Explanation of how they are organized, cataloged, and circulated.

6. **Understanding the kinds and the uses of indexes and lists for locating poetry, plays, biography, short stories, essays, songs, and other materials in collections.**

    6. (a) Discussion of the importance of indexes in locating books and informational materials: the index in a book; the card catalog; the periodical indexes; indexes to poetry, plays, short stories, essays, quotations, fairy tales, and other literature in collections.

    (b) Demonstration, discussion, and practice in the use of such indexes and bibliographies as *Granger's Index to Poetry*, Van Nostrand's *Subject Index to High School Fiction*, Cook and Monro's *Short Story Index*, Haebich's *Vocations in Fact and Fiction*, Monro and Cook's *Costume Index*, the Rue indexes, West's *Play Index*, Baker and Packman's *Guide to Best Fiction*, Cook's *Fiction Catalog*, Brewton's *Index to Children's Poetry*, Ottemiller's *Index to Plays in Collections*, the *Biography Index*, and others as need for their use arises.

CHART 4. LOCATING AND USING CURRENT MATERIALS

Desirable Learnings for Pupils	*Action Recommendations for Teachers and Librarians*
1. Understanding the value of current materials as sources of information.	1.(a) Teacher-pupil exploration and examination of magazines, newspapers, pamphlets, clippings, pictures, bulletins, and other current materials available in the school library.
	(b) Instruction of pupils in the location, arrangement and use of the clipping, pamphlet, and picture files in the library.
	(c) Provision for teaching pupils how to use lists, bibliographies, and sources of free and inexpensive materials; how to order, acquire, evaluate, and use ephemeral materials as sources of information.
2. Developing interest and facility in reading a variety of magazines.	2.(a) Introduction and evaluation of appropriate magazines.
	(b) Teacher-pupil discussion of different types of magazines: pictorial, scientific, news, literary, and others.
	(c) Provision of time and opportunity for pupils to read, enjoy, and discuss a number of magazines and to become thoroughly acquainted with their special features.
	(d) Instruction in reading current materials in order to interpret, evaluate, and utilize the information found in periodicals.
	(e) Provision of methods of classroom instruction that encourage the use of periodicals.
3. Acquiring understanding and skill in the use of periodicals and newspaper indexes for finding information in magazines and newspapers.	3.(a) Instructing pupils in the use of *Readers' Guide to Periodical Literature* with emphasis on such aspects as frequency of publication, cumulation features, magazines indexed, alphabetical arrangement—articles listed by author and sometimes by title and subject; information under each entry, including author, title of the article, name of magazine in which article appears, volume number, page, and date.
	(b) Discussion of and practice in using the *Readers' Guide* and other available newspaper and periodical indexes to locate needed information on current problems.

4. Facility in using and evaluating newspapers as sources of information.

4. (a) Providing pupils with many opportunities to examine and evaluate several newspapers, both local and national. Discussion of such aspects as coverage, special features, editorial policy, ownership, possible bias in reporting the news, advertising policies.

(b) Opportunities for pupils to use newspapers, to read and discuss the news, to analyze propaganda, to evaluate sources, to use information skillfully.

CHART 5. USING REFERENCE BOOKS TO FIND INFORMATION

Desirable Learnings for Pupils	*Action Recommendations for Teachers and Librarians*
1. Knowledge of and ability to use reference books that supply concise information about places, things, events, people, and progress.	1.(a) Provision of schedules and organization for instructing pupils when they need information which is contained in reference books and books of general information. Instruction should emphasize the scope, arrangement, and use of each reference book.
	(b) Teacher-pupil discussion of the appropriate reference books to use on given problems prior to sending pupils to the library.
2. Ability to use general encyclopedias efficiently in locating and gathering information.	2.(a) Instruction and demonstration by teachers and librarian of the use of general encyclopedias: their scope, arrangement, contents, illustrations, indexes, cross references, letter guides and other mechanical aids, and special features.
	(b) Discussion of when to use encyclopedias and for what purposes.
	(c) Provision for practice in finding desired information.
3. Ability to use handbooks, almanacs, yearbooks, manuals, and directories in locating current statistical information.	3.(a) Introduction and demonstration of the use of such reference books as *World Almanac, Information Please Almanac, Statesman's Year-Book, Statistical Abstract of the United States,* and others as sources of concise information on government, farming, industry, commerce, people, current happenings in every field of human endeavor.
	(b) Practice in their use under careful guidance.
4. Ability to use appropriate reference books in securing information on special subjects and in special fields.	4.(a) Teacher-pupil discussion of reference books useful in special fields: English, social studies, art, music, science, history, social science, and vocations. Instruction and demonstration of these books by the teachers in the content fields as pupils need to use them.
	(b) Development by the librarian of lists of reference books in special fields for the use of both teachers and pupils.

5. Understanding of how to use atlases and gazetteers, and skill in using them to locate places and secure statistical geographical information.	5.(a) Instruction in the use of atlases and geographical dictionaries with emphasis on the location of place names and statistics of population.
	(b) Instruction in the use of different kinds of atlases: geographical, political, historical.
	(c) Instruction in using maps and atlases to find a glossary of geographical terms; maps of the earth and solar system; maps of airways and world exploration; tables of oceans, seas, mountains, climate, religions, races, resources; explanations of various types of projections.

CHART 6. LOCATING AND USING INFORMATION ABOUT PEOPLE

Desirable Learnings for Pupils	*Action Recommendations for Teachers and Librarians*
1. Understanding of the great variety of sources of information about the lives of people, and facility in choosing the source appropriate to the purposes of the reader.	1.(a) Acquainting pupils with a variety of biographies and helping them locate both individual and collective biographies on the library shelves.
	(b) Teacher-pupil discussion of the purpose and value of reading biography and the selection and use of biographical information.
	(c) Examination of the many different sources of biographical information: books, dictionaries, encyclopedias, periodicals, directories, and yearbooks.
	(d) Practice in selecting the appropriate sources of information about a person, emphasizing such aspects as deciding on the kind and scope of biographical information desired and the best sources to use for obtaining it.
2. Knowledge about general biographical dictionaries and encyclopedias and facility in their use.	2. Introduction of general biographical dictionaries and aids such as Webster's *Biographical Dictionary, Dictionary of American Biography, Current Biography, Who's Who in America, Who Was Who,* and many others. Instruction should include such aspects as the scope, arrangement, text material, and abbreviations, and frequency of publication.

3. Knowledge of and ability to use the many special biographical cyclopedias, dictionaries, and directories that give concise information about men and women, living and dead, who have made significant contributions in many fields of endeavor—art, music, science, literature, government, industry, commerce.

3. (a) Demonstration of the use of biographical dictionaries to find short accounts of the lives of outstanding people in many specialized fields of endeavor—Thompson's *The International Cyclopedia of Music and Musicians*; Kunitz and Haycraft's *American Authors* and *Twentieth Century Authors*; Fielding's *Dictionary of American Painters*; Gilbert's *Who's Who in American Art*; *The Official Congressional Directory*; and others available in the school library.

(b) Demonstration and practice in locating and selecting pertinent information about people in these reference books, using such questions as: What does one like to know about people? What kind of information is to be selected? How is it to be organized?

CHART 7. USING DICTIONARIES TO FIND INFORMATION ABOUT WORDS

Desirable Learnings for Pupils

Action Recommendations for Teachers and Librarians

1. Identification of the letters of the alphabet and skill in alphabetizing.

1. (a) Introduction, explanation, and identification of the letters of the English alphabet. Teaching the order of the letters as a preliminary skill essential in using dictionaries, encyclopedias, and other materials arranged alphabetically.

   (b) Introduction of alphabet books and picture dictionaries for children.

2. Ability to use dictionaries to obtain information about words: their definition, spelling, syllabication, pronunciation, derivation, usage, and etymology.

2. (a) Explanation to pupils of what dictionaries tell about words, including pronunciation, spelling, syllabication, derivation, etymology, definition, synonyms, etc.

   (b) Instruction in looking up words in the dictionary.

   (c) Explanation of the differences between abridged and unabridged dictionaries, with emphasis on such special features as gazetteers, obsolete words, foreign words and phrases, divided pages, special plates, pictorial illustrations, number of entries.

   (d) Practice in using dictionaries.

3. Ability to use wordbooks and supplementary English language sources in gaining facility in speaking and writing.

3. Introduction and discussion of books dealing with the history and use of words: usage, synonyms, abbreviations, slang, pronunciation, rhyme, foreign terms and comparative language. Such books as the following are suggested: Fernald's *Synonyms, Antonyms, and Prepositions*; Shankle's *Current Abbreviations*; Partridge's Usage and Abusage; Colby's *American Pronouncing Dictionary of Troublesome Words*; Walker's *Rhyming Dictionary*; and many others.

4. Ability to use foreign language dictionaries.

4. Discussion of foreign language dictionaries with pupils who need to use them in foreign language courses. Emphasize their scope, arrangement, treatment, and use.

CHART 8. LOCATING AND GATHERING INFORMATION FROM MANY SOURCES

Desirable Learnings for Pupils	*Action Recommendations for Teachers and Librarians*
1. Ability to determine what information is needed and the appropriate sources for locating and gathering it.	**1.** Pupil-teacher discussion of what information is needed on a problem or subject and where it may be found. The following questions are useful: What do we already know about the problem, the topic, the question? What more do we need to know? Can we get information from people, from TV or radio? Can we go to local sources of information—to social, governmental, or civic agencies; industries; museums; service organizations; travel bureaus? Can we use books, films, pictures, pamphlets, magazines? What do we have in the school library? On the particular problem under study which sources appear most promising?
2. Acquiring facility in observation and the ability to learn from direct experience.	**2.(a)** Teacher-pupil planning of field trips when a real need arises for gathering first-hand information on a problem.
	(b) Instruction on how to observe, including such questions as: What is the purpose of our proposed field trip? What, in general, do we expect to see? What questions do we want answered? How shall we take notes so that specific information will not be forgotten? How will the information be recorded? How shall we evaluate the experience?
3. Ability to listen and to learn from the experience.	**3.(a)** Pupil-teacher discussion of what constitutes effective listening. Explanation and demonstration of a variety of purposes: listening to explore, to evaluate, to observe social amenities. Suggestions for organizing and remembering information gained in conversation.
	(b) Provision for practice in skillful listening as one means of gaining information and knowledge.
4. Ability to interview and to use people as important, useful, and authoritative resources.	**4.** Discussion and demonstration of interviewing techniques. The following suggestions are useful: decide what questions you want answered; make sure the person to be interviewed is reliable and has access to the information; examine your own biases about the subject before the interview; prepare a tentative list of questions that you wish answered; phrase questions clearly; be concise in getting to the point; listen carefully; record all information at your earliest convenience.

5. Ability to locate and use all kinds of printed and audio-visual materials in libraries, museums, galleries, and institutions.

5. Instruction in locating information in the library and in using library tools and library resources as outlined on preceding pages.

6. Ability to read with understanding, to choose pertinent and appropriate materials.

6. Librarian-pupil discussion of procedures such as deciding first what you are looking for, choosing books and materials appropriate to the problem, skimming through material first to find out if information is pertinent. Rereading and taking notes.

7. Ability to record the sources of information in approved bibliographical form.

7. Instruction in making a bibliography including: its purpose; the definition of the items to be included; the form to use; the data to be included—the author, title, publisher, copyright date, and pages. Special rules to follow in listing magazines and other nonbook materials.

8. Ability to quote authority and record sources of information in footnotes.

8. (a) Explanation and demonstration of how to make footnotes. Emphasis on such points as citing authority; recording exact sources; acknowledging indebtedness; using correct form; explanation of special abbreviations used.

(b) Helping pupils use the directions and suggestions presented in textbooks, hand-books, and style books on how to record the sources of information.

(c) Practice with guidance in recording sources of information, followed by evalua-tion of achievement in the methods of inquiry.

CHART 9. ORGANIZING INFORMATION—OUTLINING AND NOTE-TAKING

Desirable Learnings for Pupils	*Action Recommendations for Teachers and Librarians*
1. Ability to select information pertinent to a problem.	1.(a) Presentation and demonstration by teacher or librarian of the procedural steps in organizing information: making a plan for selecting information before starting to read; deciding what kind of information is sought, what kinds of questions need to be answered; considering how the information is to be used and for what specific purpose; reading the selection through quickly to decide what the author is talking about and whether the information is appropriate to the problem; reading again for answers to the questions that have been formulated; trying to identify the topic sentence in each paragraph; looking for the key words that support the idea in the topic sentence; using any marginal topics in deciding what the important ideas are in the selection.
	(b) Provision of many opportunities for pupils to read and organize information under the guidance of teachers and librarians in many situations at all grade levels.
	(c) Pupil-teacher discussion of the importance of selecting and organizing information.
2. Ability to organize information.	2. Presentation and demonstration by teachers and librarians of the procedural steps in outlining: making a list, before beginning to read, of the questions or topics about which information is needed and under which information can be organized; reading and selecting information pertinent to the topics or questions; recording selected information under appropriate headings (this single operation may be defined as note-taking); adding new topics discovered in the reading that had not been previously thought of; adding subtopics if the amount of information warrants; examining the main topics or ideas to determine the most logical arrangement in relation to the subject of study; listing first the most important topic; listing others closely related.

3. Ability to take notes and record sources.

4. Ability to organize information gained from observation and listening.

3. (a) Demonstration by teacher and pupils of ways to take effective notes using such steps as reading a paragraph aloud for the main ideas; recording these ideas on separate cards or sheets of paper under topics similar to those chosen in outlining; underscoring the main ideas using telegraphic style of recording; giving credit for any exact words used by enclosing in quotation marks when quoting directly; citing authority and source—the author, title, publisher, date of publication, and exact page from which material has been taken; rearranging notes from various sources in logical sequence.

(b) Practice in taking notes in many situations, and continued evaluation of progress.

(c) Demonstration and discussion of bibliographical procedures and practice in recording sources in appropriate form.

4. Pupil-teacher discussion of means of selecting and organizing information as one listens or observes. Understanding that the same general steps can be pursued in these activities as in reading.

CHART 10. ANALYZING, INTERPRETING, EVALUATING INFORMATION

Desirable Learnings for Pupils	*Action Recommendations for Teachers and Librarians*
1. Ability to read for meaning —to understand what is read.	1. Continuous reading guidance in all content subjects, with explanations of new concepts and terms and of the meaning of new words or specialized vocabulary. Explanation of the techniques required for reading different kinds of materials for different purposes.
2. Ability to evaluate the sources of information.	2. Pupil-teacher discussion of such questions as: Is the information true or false? Is the author known to be reliable? When or how did he record the information? Did he go to original sources? Did he record from memory or is it an account of his own direct experiences? Is he known to be an authority in the field about which he is writing? What is his general point of view? What are his motives in giving the information? If he represents an institution or organization, for what does it stand? What is the recency of the information? If the information comes from periodicals or newspapers, what is the policy of the editors, their integrity, reliability, and possible bias?
3. Ability to differentiate between fact and opinion.	3. Opportunities for pupils to differentiate between fact and opinion, to understand that opinion is what a person *thinks* about the things he observes, reads about, or experiences directly; that opinion is influenced by the person's culture patterns, his values and beliefs; that more than one opinion may be justified; that facts can be checked and evaluated.
4. Ability to recognize and evaluate propaganda.	4.(a) Practice in the evaluation of informational materials, using such questions and checks as the following: Does the author differentiate between fact and opinion? Does he use power words to develop emotional reactions? Does he attempt to confuse the issue? Is there omission of important aspects of pertinent information? Does he use such techniques as assigning scapegoats; name-calling; broad, glittering generalities; testimonials; band-wagon exhortation?
	(b) Discussion and use of propaganda materials to identify propaganda and demonstrate how it is used; analysis of cartoons and speeches; comparison of newspaper articles, editorials, headlines that report and discuss the same facts.

5. Ability to identify time and place relationships, as well as causal relationships, in series of facts and ideas. Understanding that this is a crucial factor in analysis and interpretation of information and knowledge.

5. (a) Practice in arranging organized information, recognizing pertinent relationships, considering possible causes and their relationship to effects.

(b) Teacher-pupil discussion of methods of evaluating information, repeated in many situations, with consideration of classroom activities and the maturity of pupils.

CHART 11. UTILIZING INFORMATION—DISCUSSION, PROBLEM-SOLVING, AND REPORTING

Desirable Learnings for Pupils

1. Facility in summarizing information, making generalizations, and reaching conclusions on the basis of available evidence.

2. Facility in using information to solve problems and make decisions, to think deductively as well as procedurally.

3. Ability to report, to share information.

Action Recommendations for Teachers and Librarians

1.(a) Demonstration by teachers in many classroom situations of the process involved in generalizing from information. The teachers may use a series of questions to explain how it is done: What possible generalizations or conclusions can I draw from my interpretation of the information (or problem)? Which ones appear untenable? Do I have enough information to warrant conclusions and generalizations? Have I taken into account my own possible bias or point of view in reaching this conclusion? What are possible alternatives? What is likely to eventuate as a result of these conclusions?

(b) Classroom instruction that encourages and demands the practice of these skills, rather than instruction that requires only the recall of facts.

(c) Continuous practice of these skills by pupils, followed by evaluation.

2. Pupil-teacher discussion of ways in which information is used in problem-solving and decision-making. Such questions as the following are useful: What does the information mean to me? What conclusions can I reach? Would these conclusions be useful in other situations? What should I believe on the basis of these conclusions? What should I do? How can I use this information? (There should be clarification of the fact that all conclusions do not necessarily entail action. They may provide the individual with different ways of thinking and believing.)

3. Helping students to report information adequately with emphasis on: a clear statement of the topic or problem; a statement of the most important points; a statement of sources of information; summary and conclusions.

4. Facility in the techniques of discussion.

4. (a) Defining and clarifying the purposes of discussion with emphasis on such statements as the following: discussion is sharing facts and conclusions and permitting the information to be subjected to critical analysis; discussion is a cooperative effort to arrive at facts or conclusions about a subject; discussion starts only after a careful and open-minded search for facts.

(b) Evaluating a specific discussion: Was it an expression of opinion, a *'tis—'tisn't* exchange, or were facts used to support opinion? Was it a debate or were there attempts to arrive at a compromise? Did the discussion result in a conclusion, a plan, a change in thinking or attitude?

(c) Pupil participation in discussion followed by *evaluation* and *identification* of procedures used, so that *skill* in discussion is taught deliberately. Evaluation should include, therefore, judgment about the *content* of the discussion, and also the *process*.

5. Understanding the difference between memorizing facts and using information and knowledge.

5. Summarization and evaluation of the process involved in bringing facts to bear on problems, utilizing information in decision-making, weighing the evidence and changing or clarifying values and beliefs as the evidence comes in—procedures that tend to promote logical thinking and effective behavior. (This is teaching for transfer.)

Evaluating the Skills

Two questions have to be answered by a school staff in judging the effectiveness of a skill development program: (1) How well do our pupils select, organize, and utilize the knowledge and information? (2) *Can* and do they read with enthusiasm? Both questions are pertinent since they represent the interrelated and interdependent objectives of the reading guidance program. Both questions yield no simple, easy answers.

What makes the evaluation of the learning skills so difficult? First, one must take into account the long-term skill development of the individual. Evaluation at a single given point in skill development is not too effective a measure, since the acid test of achievement in these skills is the degree to which the individual uses reading for lifelong learning, for gathering information, for solving problems and making decisions, as well as for entertainment and fulfillment. Tests of prediction are not easily developed nor are pencil and paper tests at present available.

Assuming that a program can be evaluated only in terms of stated objectives, one is faced with a second complicating factor inherent in the objectives of skill development. Since skill development is directed toward *ways of doing* rather than in memorizing a body of knowledge, it follows that any evaluation procedures must attempt not only to give some approximation of how well the individual knows the particulars of the skills, but, of even greater importance, to indicate how well he performs them.

The problem of *what is to be evaluated* can be defined quite simply. Can pupils perform the following tasks:

Identify the information they need that is pertinent to a given problem?

Decide on the kinds of library materials needed?

Use the card catalog to find appropriate books?

Go to the proper shelves and choose a number of books which may contain sought-for information?

Select proper topics to search for in the index in the book and find pages on which information is to be found?

Skim the material to see if it is adequate?

Read and take adequate notes, organize information, and reach conclusions?

Bring the new information to bear on their problems?

Make a bibliography of materials and sources?

If an affirmative answer can be given to these questions, it is assumed that pupils know the particulars of the skill required in locating information in books.

The point of difficulty for the teacher and librarian is not *what* is to be evaluated, but *how* these skills are to be detected, how judged on the basis of performance.

Evaluative Procedures and Study Instruments

Here it seems fair to assume that reliance should not be placed on a single method of evaluation, but that a combination of procedures should be used, procedures that take into account the needs of the particular pupils, that motivate continued learnings, and check present progress. A number of promising evaluation practices may be mentioned.

1. Many test instruments and study forms that are designed to test the person's ability to read with understanding and to use the sources of information are available. Among many reliable ones are the standard tests published by Science Research Associates. The *S.R.A. Reading Record* measures map-table-graph reading and index usage as well as general reading comprehension. The *Iowa Every-Pupil Test of Basic Skills* is widely used.

Authorities in the field of the social studies have developed a number of test instruments in critical thinking that serve to test the individual's ability to obtain and organize facts, to draw conclusions, and apply generalizations. Test forms have been produced for use in the primary grades as well as high school. As inventory instruments, these are all extremely useful in giving the teacher and librarian a fairly accurate picture of the pupil's ability to use maps, charts, and reference books, and to interpret and utilize information.

Many of the instructional manuals on teaching the use of books and libraries contain exercises, drills, and practice tests. It might be mentioned that teachers and librarians find it a salutary experience to take a battery of these tests themselves before embarking on a program of skill development for their pupils.[3]

2. A second major method of evaluating skills is for teachers to check continuously on the pupil's ability to employ or use the skills. For example, the best test of the child's ability to use the *Readers' Guide to Periodical Literature* is his success in finding needed information in current magazines. The best check on his achievement in the organizational skills is how well the pupil takes notes, outlines materials, constructs graphs, reads maps, reads directions. These procedures not only provide a check on the pupil's present skill development, but furnish practice for him in perfecting the skills.

3. Continuous, careful observation of the work produced by the student provides a third means of checking on skill development. If his written and oral reports are well organized, if he has evaluated his sources, detected possible bias, reached conclusions based on the facts, one may assume that he is becoming habituated to the use of the "learning skills." The need to check the work produced suggests, moreover, that the assessment of the pupil's skill cannot be separated from the appraisal of what he has learned. Carried to a logical conclusion, observation of the pupil's

[3] Among the many useful instruments the following are cited:

Iowa Test of Educational Development, Test 9: Use of Sources of Information. Chicago: Science Research Associates, 1954.

T. L. Kelly and others. *Stanford Achievement Test,* Test 9: Study Skills Test. Stanford, Calif.: Stanford University Press, 1951.

H. L. Spitzer and others. *Iowa Every-Pupil Test of Basic Skills,* Elementary Test B, Work-Study Skills (grades 3-5); Advanced Test B, Work-Study Skills (grades 5-9). Chicago: Science Research Associates, 1952.

Henry T. Tyler and George C. Kimber. *Tyler-Kimber Study Skills Test.* Stanford, Calif.: Stanford University Press, 1951.

Goodwin Watson and E. M. Glaser. *Watson-Glaser Critical Thinking Appraisal* (High School and College). New York: World Book Co., 1952.

J. W. Wrightstone. *Tests of Critical Thinking in the Social Studies: Elementary School Series.* New York: Bureau of Publications, Teachers College, Columbia University, 1942.

achievement in the content subjects is valid evaluation of his skill development.

4. Still another promising source of information is the pupil's own evaluation of progress. It is a wise teacher who constantly encourages the pupil to use such questions as: How well have I done this? What blocks me? Can I improve? How? Perhaps no other learning is more important to the child than the ability to evaluate objectively his own accomplishments, to ascertain what is wrong, to detect the precise areas in which he is weak and then to plan for his own continued learning.

5. Lastly, the librarian or teacher may ask, With what interest and enthusiasm does the pupil read? The acceptance of the idea that skill and interest in reading are not only interdependent and interrelated but inseparable leads inevitably to the conclusion that the pupil's interest and taste in reading will mount as his "skill" increases. Illogical as it might be for a school staff to try to establish causal relationships between skill development and library circulation figures or the number of titles on individual reading records, it seems fair to assume that these data provide some evidence of both reading interest and skill. Equally pertinent as evidence would be the reactions of parents to the pupils' leisure reading, while the quality of academic achievement in the school and the general morale of students would certainly give some general assessment of the school's reading program since reading retardation and academic failure are highly correlated.

Evaluation that demands continuous observation by teachers and librarians is time consuming and often frustrating. It does not lend itself to neat scores and percentages. Yet improvement in any area of the school's program starts and continues with a painstaking attempt to evaluate achievement.

Looking Ahead

Because there are no tests that measure reading interest and reading habits, and little research to direct a school staff along the road in a total school approach to reading guidance, experimentation based on a maze of hunches, assumptions, and untested practices and procedures must continue.

There is urgent need to convert the wealth of good intentions and ideas relating to the guidance of reading into action. Such an undertaking calls for teachers informed about reading materials and diligent in their attempts to help youth become skillful users of books and other media of communication. It implies the expansion of school library facilities and invokes the services of librarians who are teachers of children, not just custodians of books. It demands concerted planning, tryout, evaluation, and possible replanning by a school staff which is concerned about the guidance of youth.

The success of the undertaking will be judged by the reading behavior of the generation which is the product of such teaching. If the future belongs to the educated man, and if formal education is the starting point—not the termination—of education, it follows that the school must instill in youth a drive toward continued learning and the skills to make the learnings operate in their lives.

And if the future also belongs to automation and civil defense, it is possible that school programs which emphasize the qualities of mind, imagination, and spirit may be of more transcendent value than vocational and air-age education, essential as these are. The teachers of youth should be inspired by the certain knowledge that the "products of teaching are influenced largely by what is emphasized." And, as the struggle of ideologies and values continues, it follows that reading guidance programs need to provide for ever-increasing numbers of youth the ability to garner "bright images" from books and print, the skill to think logically, and the will to participate effectively in a democratic society.

PROBLEMS FOR DISCUSSION AND STUDY

1. Examine a curriculum guide which suggests curriculum content in broad areas for an eighth-grade class in social studies, science, or English. Sketch in outline form the skills that pupils need in the use of books and libraries in relation to the suggested curriculum content.

2. Make a plan for helping teachers in a school to acquire information about library resources. Suggest a number of ways to help them keep informed about current books as well as other learning materials.

3. If you agree with the approach to the teaching of the learning skills presented in preceding chapters, what might you plan to do in your own school situation about improving the teaching of the learning skills?

4. Assume for purposes of study that a twelfth-grade English class is required to do a research paper on some subject of individual interest. The teacher has asked you, the librarian, to come into the classroom to teach pupils how to carry on the research for the project and how to make a bibliography. Outline your lesson.

5. Collect and examine a number of pencil tests for evaluating mastery of the work-study skills. Which ones would you recommend for use in an elementary school? A high school?

6. You may wish to prepare self-teaching materials that could be used by high school pupils in orientation to the school library and in the use of all of its resources.

Suggested Aids and Tools

Aldrich, Ella V. *Using Books and Libraries.* New York: Prentice-Hall, 1951.

Alexander, Carter, and Burke, A. J. *How to Locate Educational Information and Data.* New York: Bureau of Publications, Teachers College, Columbia University, 1950.

Arps, Louise W. *Speaking of Books.* Denver: Denver Public Schools, 1941.

Berner, Elsa R. *Integrating Library Instruction with Classroom Teaching at Plainview Junior High School.* Chicago: American Library Association, 1958.

Boyd, Jessie and others. *Books, Libraries and You.* New York: Charles Scribner's Sons, 1949.

Cleary, Florence Damon. *Library in Action.* Detroit: Board of Education, 1941.

Cook, Margaret G. *The New Library Key: An Aid in Using Books and Libraries,* 7th ed. New York: H. W. Wilson Co., 1956.

Cundiff, Ruby Ethel. *Recommended Reference Books for the High School Library,* 3d ed. Chicago: Wilcox and Follett Co., 1949.

Dent, Charles H. *Bulletin Boards for Teaching.* Austin: University of Texas, 1955.

Grambs, Jean D. *Using Current Materials to Study Current Problems.* Stanford, Calif.: Stanford University Press, 1952.

Hook, Lucyle and Gaver, M. V. *The Research Paper.* New York: Prentice-Hall, 1952.

Ingles, May and McCague, Anna. *Teaching the Use of Books and Libraries.* New York: H. W. Wilson Co., 1944.

Marjarum, Edward W. *How to Use a Book.* New Brunswick, N.J.: Rutgers University Press, 1947.

Metropolitan School Study Council. *Five Steps to Reading Success in Science, Social Studies, and Mathematics.* New York: Metropolitan School Study Council, 1954.

Morse, Horace T. and McCune, George H. *Selected Items for Testing of Study Skills.* Washington, D.C.: National Council for the Social Studies, 1949.

Mott, Carolyne and Baisden, Leo B. *Children's Book on How to Use Books and Libraries.* New York: Charles Scribner's Sons, 1955.

Orchard, Norris E. *Study Successfully; Eighteen Keys to Better Work.* New York: McGraw-Hill Book Co., 1953.

Rossoff, Martin. *Using Your High School Library.* New York: H. W. Wilson Co., 1952.

Russell, Harold G. and others. *The Use of Books and Libraries,* 8th ed. Minneapolis: University of Minnesota Library, 1955.

Santa, Beauel M. and others. *How to Use the Library.* Palo Alto, Calif.: Pacific Books, 1955.

Scripture, Elizabeth and Greer, Margaret R. *Find it Yourself,* 4th ed. New York: H. W. Wilson Co., 1955.

Spache, George D. and Berg, Paul C. *The Art of Efficient Reading.* New York: Macmillan Co., 1955.

Strang, Ruth M. *Guided Study and Homework.* Washington, D.C.: National Education Association. 1955.

Toser, Marie A. *Library Manual: A Study-Work Manual on the Use of Books and Libraries,* 5th ed. New York: H. W. Wilson Co., 1955.

Walraven, Margaret Kessler and Hall-Quest, Alfred. *Teaching Through the Elementary School Library.* New York: H. W. Wilson Co., 1948.

Witty, Paul A. *How to Become a Better Reader.* Chicago: Science Research Associates, 1953.

Witty, Paul A. *How to Improve Your Reading.* Chicago: Science Research Associates, 1956.

Wrenn, Gilbert and Larsen, Robert P. *Studying Effectively,* 2d ed. Stanford, Calif.: Leland Stanford Junior University, 1955.

INDEX